STEP BY STEP
VEGETARIAN
COOKBOOK

STEP BY STEP
VEGETARIAN
COOKBOOK

Chris Hardisty

PARRAGON

CONTENTS

The publishers would like to thank the following people who supplied recipes and without whom this book would not have been possible: Chris Hardisty, Rosie Brook, Pam Knutson, Freda Hooker, Pauline Robertshaw, D.M. Arnot, Val Shaw, Brian Holmes, Vivien Margison, Isabel Wilson, Marianne Vaney, Ian Jones, Wendy Godden, Joan Davis, Jo Wright, Isabel Booth, Alison Ray, Susan Mills, Kate Allen, Pat McGlashan, Deirdre Kuntz, Suzanne Ross, Joan Davies, Merle Millan, Ann Bohren, Winifred Allen, Sumitra Gopal and Sally Halon.

Photography by Peter Barry
Food prepared and styled by Helen Burdett
Designed by Claire Leighton and Judith Chant
Typesetting and graphics by Julie Smith
Edited by Jillian Stewart

3071
© 1993 Coombe Books
This edition published in 1993 by Coombe Books for
Parragon Book Service Ltd,
707 High Street, Finchley, London N12 0BT
All rights reserved
Printed and bound in Singapore
ISBN 1-85813-420-X

INTRODUCTION

There's a revolution taking place – a food revolution. A decade or so ago vegetarians were seen as weirdos, now everybody knows one and almost four million of us are one. The numbers are growing so fast – doubled in the past year – that before long, carnivores will only be able to do it with other consenting adults in private.

The scale of change is extraordinary. The results of a major Vegetarian Society food survey, carried out by Bradford University, shows that apart from 28,000 becoming vegetarian every week, over 4½ million people eat no red meat and over 9 million have drastically reduced their meat intake. And if that isn't dramatic enough, 40 per cent of the population have considered becoming vegetarian.

People come to vegetarianism for different reasons: some out of compassion for animals, mostly reared in appalling conditions and slaughtered barbarically; some out of environmental concern; some because of Third-World impoverishment; and others for reasons of health.

Vegetarians have lower rates of obesity, and suffer less from coronary heart disease, high blood pressure, cancer of the bowel and a host of other disorders than their meat-eating counterparts. The professional debate isn't any longer about whether vegetarians are healthier than meat eaters, but why they are! Even the government's own health advisers recommend that we cut down on fats generally and in particular saturated fats by substituting them with polyunsaturated fats; that we reduce salt and sugar intake and increase fibre and complex carbohydrates.

In simple language this means that we should cut down on meat and animal products and eat more fresh vegetables and fruit; include plenty of bread, pasta, rice, pulses, grains and potatoes in our meals and keep processed foods to a minimum. In fact, what they're describing is a vegetarian diet! The World Health Organisation goes even further than this and recommends – albeit in polite and very guarded language – that meat should now be considered an optional extra.

There are thousands of ingredients from around the world that most meat-eaters simply ignore, but which can open up a whole new taste experience. Across India and the East millions of people eat nothing but vegetarian food, while the Japanese diet contains very little meat, and traditional African and Middle Eastern foods are largely meat-free.

So what's the outcome of this move towards vegetarianism? Millions of people reluctantly munching away at muesli and lentil burgers, hating every minute of it? Not a bit! As this book is about to reveal to you, vegetarian eating is about imagination and experimentation, diversity and change. Start to look beyond the 'something and two veg', use your imagination and you will discover dishes more delicious than you ever dreamed.

The Vegetarian Society only endorses the use of free-range eggs and vegetarian cheeses (those made with non-animal rennet) and although it was once difficult to find anything other than vegetarian Cheddar you will now find a large selection of vegetarian cheeses in health food stores, so try to use these wherever possible.

Our choice of food has enormous influence not only on our health, but on the lives of others and on the earth itself. And it all starts here!

JULIET GELLATLEY
THE VEGETARIAN SOCIETY

SNACKS & STARTERS

Vegetarian snacks and starters offer endless opportunities for the cook to use his or her imaginative flair – whether it's a salad, stuffed vegetables, or a risotto, the scope is limitless. It is always best to look on any snack or starter as a mini main course where garnishing and presentation are concerned. This applies to the starter in particular, as it introduces the meal and should give a taste of things to come.

Starters can consist of almost anything you wish to serve as long it does not clash with the main course. Try to balance a substantial main dish with a light starter and vice versa. Many main dishes can be served in small portions as starters, or as snacks. Pay attention to the ingredients and try not to duplicate them in the first course and the main dish. For example, if your main course does not include raw food, serve a mixed salad, or if your main dish is salad based, serve a hot starter such as soup.

Home-made soups are delicious, and as well as being the perfect starter, the heartier ones can be served with bread as a one-course meal. Making soup was once thought to be fiddly and time-consuming. Not so now with the aid of a liquidiser, although if you do not have one it is possible to press the soup through a sieve to produce a creamy soup. Most vegetables are suitable for use in soups, so this is a perfect way of using up almost any ingredients you may have to hand. Soup also keeps well and often tastes better the day after it has been cooked!

FENNEL AND WALNUT SOUP

*A delicious and unusual combination makes this
soup perfect for special occasions.*

SERVES 4

1 bulb chopped fennel
1 head chopped celery
1 large onion, chopped
1 tbsp olive or sunflower oil
75g/3oz walnuts, crushed
1150ml/2 pints vegetable stock, bean
   stock or water
45ml/3 tbsps Pernod
140ml/¼ pint single cream
Salt and pepper
Parsley to garnish

1. Sauté the fennel, celery and onion in the oil over a low heat.

2. Add the walnuts and stock and simmer for half an hour.

3. Liquidise the simmered ingredients together and return to the pan.

4. Add the Pernod, single cream and salt and pepper.

5. Reheat gently and serve garnished with parsley.

TIME: Preparation takes about 15 minutes, cooking takes about 1 hour 10 minutes.

SERVING IDEA: Celery leaves may be used as a garnish if no parsley is available.

VARIATION: Other nuts such as cashews or almonds may be used in place of walnuts.

WATCHPOINT: Do not allow the soup to boil after adding the cream and Pernod.

CREAM OF CARROT SOUP

A classic soup which is suitable for any occasion.

SERVES 4

1 large onion, chopped
2 cloves garlic, crushed
1 tbsp olive oil
450g/1lb carrots, chopped
1 tsp mixed herbs
850ml/1½ pints stock
140ml/¼ pint soured cream
Salt and pepper

1. Sauté the chopped onion and garlic in the oil until transparent.

2. Add the carrots, mixed herbs and stock.

3. Bring to the boil and simmer for about 30 minutes until the carrots are soft.

4. Cool a little and then liquidise until smooth.

5. Add the soured cream, season to taste and mix thoroughly.

6. Heat through gently and serve.

TIME: Preparation takes about 10 minutes, cooking takes 35 minutes.

WATCHPOINT: Do not allow the soup to boil after adding the soured cream.

VARIATION: For a richer soup, omit the soured cream and add a swirl of double cream just before serving.

WILD RICE SOUP

A meal in itself when served with granary bread and a green salad.

SERVES 4

50g/2oz wild rice
420ml/¾ pint water
2 onions, chopped
1 tbsp butter or ghee
2 sticks celery, chopped
½ tsp dried thyme
½ tsp dried sage
850ml/1½ pints water or vegetable stock
2 tsps Vecon (vegetable stock)
1 tbsp shoyu (Japanese soy sauce)
6 small potatoes, peeled and roughly
  chopped
1 carrot, finely diced
Milk or single cream

---

1. Add the wild rice to the water, bring to the boil, reduce the heat and simmer for 40-50 minutes until the rice has puffed and most of the liquid has been absorbed.

2. Sauté the onions in the butter until transparent.

3. Add the celery, thyme and sage and cook for 5-10 minutes.

4. Add the water, vecon, shoyu and potatoes.

5. Simmer for 20 minutes or until the potatoes are cooked.

6. Blend the mixture in a liquidiser until smooth.

7. Return to the pan, add the carrot and wild rice.

8. Add the milk or cream to thin the soup to the desired consistency.

9. Reheat gently and serve.

TIME: Preparation takes about 15 minutes. Cooking takes 30 minutes plus 40 minutes to cook the wild rice.

COOK'S TIP: You can prepare and cook the soup whilst the wild rice is cooking. Add the rice to the soup at the end of the cooking time.

FREEZING: Cook a large quantity of wild rice and freeze in small portions. Add to the soup or other dishes as needed.

VARIATION: Toast some flaked almonds and sprinkle on top of the soup before serving.

MISO SOUP

This delicious soup of Japanese origin makes a nice change for a starter.

SERVES 2

1 small onion, grated
2.5cm/¾-inch fresh root ginger, peeled
  and finely chopped
1 clove garlic, crushed
1 tbsp sesame oil
1 carrot, peeled and finely sliced
¼ small cauliflower, divided into florets
1150ml/2 pints water
1 large tbsp arame (Japanese seaweed)
25g/1oz peas (fresh or frozen)
2 tbsps shoyu (Japanese soy sauce)
1 tbsp miso (red bean paste)
Black pepper to taste
2 spring onions, finely chopped

1. Sauté the onion, ginger and garlic in the sesame oil for a few minutes.

2. Add the carrot and cauliflower and gently sweat the vegetables for 5 minutes.

3. Add the water, arame, peas and shoyu. Cook for 15-20 minutes until the vegetables are soft.

4. Blend the miso to a paste with a little of the soup liquid and add to the soup but do not allow to boil.

5. Season with freshly ground black pepper to taste.

6. Serve garnished with chopped spring onions.

TIME: Preparation takes 15 minutes, cooking takes 20 minutes.

SERVING IDEA: Serve with hot garlic bread.

VARIATION: Substitute other vegetables such as mooli, turnip, swede, mange tout or green beans but remember that this soup is mainly a broth with a few floating vegetables.

COOK'S TIP: Arame, shoyu and miso are available from Japanese grocers.

SPINACH AND APPLE SOUP

*The two main flavours complement each other
perfectly in this hearty soup.*

SERVES 4

25g/1oz butter or margarine
1 small onion, chopped
25g/1oz wholemeal flour
570ml/1 pint vegetable stock
450g/1lb spinach, shredded
225g/8oz apple purée
280ml/½ pint milk
Salt and freshly ground black pepper
Pinch of nutmeg
Lemon juice
Natural yogurt
A little parsley, finely chopped

1. Melt the butter in a large saucepan and fry the onion until soft.

2. Add the flour and cook to a roux.

3. Add the stock slowly, stir well and simmer for 10 minutes.

4. Add the spinach and cook until tender.

5. Cool slightly and mix in the apple purée.

6. Place all the ingredients in a liquidiser and blend until smooth.

7. Return to the pan and reheat slowly together with the milk.

8. Add the salt, pepper, nutmeg and lemon juice to taste.

9. Serve in individual bowls with the yogurt swirled on the top and garnished with chopped parsley.

TIME: Preparation takes 15 minutes, cooking takes 15 minutes.

COOK'S TIP: The apple purée can be omitted if not available but it adds an unusual flavour to the soup.

VARIATION: If there is no vegetable water available for the stock, a teaspoonful of Vecon (vegetable stock) or a stock cube can be mixed with 1 pint of boiling water instead.

EASY LENTIL SOUP

*A good old-fashioned soup which is sure
to please all the family.*

SERVES 4-6

225g/8oz split red lentils
25g/1oz butter or margarine
1 medium onion, peeled and finely
    chopped
2 stalks celery, finely diced
2 carrots, scrubbed and finely diced
Grated rind of 1 lemon
1150ml/2 pints light vegetable stock
Salt and freshly ground black pepper

1. Pick over the lentils and remove any stones. Rinse well.

2. Heat the butter or margarine in a pan and sauté the onion for 2-3 minutes.

3. Add the diced celery and carrots and let the vegetables sweat for 5-10 minutes.

4. Stir in the lentils, add the lemon rind, stock and salt and pepper to taste.

5. Bring to the boil, reduce the heat and simmer for 15-20 minutes until the vegetables are tender.

6. Roughly blend the soup in a liquidiser, it should not be too smooth.

7. Check the seasoning and reheat gently.

TIME: Preparation takes about 10 minutes, cooking takes 15-20 minutes.

SERVING IDEA: Sprinkle with cheese and serve with hot toast.

FREEZING: Freeze for up to 3 months.

GARDEN VEGETABLE SOUP

A hearty soup perfect for those cold winter nights.

SERVES 4-6

1 tbsp margarine
½ head fennel, finely chopped
3 medium carrots, diced
1 medium onion, chopped
2-3 cloves garlic, crushed
1 parsnip, diced
Salt and pepper
2 heaped tsps dried parsley
1 tbsp tomato purée
1 large potato, diced
1150ml/2 pints vegetable stock
50g/2oz frozen peas

1. Melt the margarine in a large pan and add the fennel, carrots, onion, garlic, parsnip and seasoning.

2. Cover and allow to 'sweat' over a very low heat for 10-15 minutes, stirring occasionally.

3. Add the parsley, tomato purée, potato and stock.

4. Stir well, bring to the boil and simmer for 20-30 minutes until the vegetables are tender.

5. Just before serving, add the frozen peas.

6. Bring back to the boil and serve immediately.

TIME: Preparation takes 15 minutes, cooking takes about 35 minutes.

SERVING IDEA: Serve with crusty rolls or French bread.

VARIATION: If fennel is not available, use 2 or 3 sticks of finely chopped celery.

SPLIT PEA SOUP

*A classic soup which looks extra special with
a swirl of yogurt on top.*

SERVES 6

225g/8oz split peas
3 pints vegetable stock or water plus a
    stock cube
50g/2oz margarine
1 large onion, chopped
3 sticks celery, chopped
2 leeks, finely sliced
2 medium potatoes, peeled and diced
1 medium carrot, finely chopped,
Salt and pepper

1. Cook the peas in the stock for 10-15
minutes.

2. Meanwhile, melt the margarine and
sauté the onion, celery and leeks for a few
minutes.

3. Add to the peas and stock together with
the potatoes and carrot and bring back to
the boil.

4. Simmer for 30 minutes.

5. Season well and liquidise until smooth.

TIME: Preparation takes about 10 minutes, cooking takes 40 minutes.

SERVING IDEA: If the vegetables are chopped small enough you can
serve this as a chunky soup.

COOK'S TIP: If you do not have a liquidiser you can pass the soup through a sieve
although it will not be quite as thick.

FRENCH ONION SOUP

*This soup tastes best if cooked the day
before it is needed and then reheated as required.*

SERVES 4

3 medium onions
50g/2oz butter or margarine
25g/1oz plain flour or soya flour
1ltr/1¾ pints boiling vegetable stock or
    water plus 2 stock cubes
Salt and pepper

Topping
4 slices French bread, cut crosswise
50g/2oz Cheddar cheese, grated
25g/1oz Parmesan cheese, grated

1. Slice the onions very finely into rings.

2. Melt the butter in a pan, add the onion
rings and fry over a medium heat until
well browned.

3. Mix in the flour and stir well until
browned.

4. Add the stock and seasoning and
simmer for 30 minutes.

5. Toast the bread on both sides.

6. Combine the cheese, and divide
between the bread slice; grill until golden
brown.

7. Place the slices of bread and cheese in
the bottom of individual soup dishes and
spoon the soup over the top.

8. Serve at once.

TIME: Preparation takes 10 minutes, cooking takes 30 minutes.

VARIATION: For a special occasion, add a tablespoonful of brandy to the stock.

WATCHPOINT: The onions must be very well browned, as this gives the rich
colour to the soup.

27

GAZPACHO

One of Spain's tastiest exports.

SERVES 4

450g/1lb ripe tomatoes
1 small onion
1 small green pepper
1 clove garlic, crushed
¼ medium cucumber
1 tbsp red wine vinegar
1 tbsp olive oil
1 x 400g/14oz can tomato juice
1-2 tbsps lime juice
Salt and pepper

1. Plunge the tomatoes into boiling water, leave for 2 minutes, then remove the skins and seeds.

2. Chop the onion and pepper and place in a liquidiser with the tomatoes, garlic, cucumber, vinegar, oil and tomato juice.

3. Purée until smooth.

4. Add the lime juice and seasoning to taste.

5. Pour the soup into a glass dish and chill until required.

TIME: Preparation takes 10 minutes.

SERVING IDEA: Serve garnished with croutons and finely diced cucumber.

WATCHPOINT: If the soup is too thick, add more tomato juice after Step 5.

VARIATION: Lemon juice may be used in place of the lime juice.

SWEET POTATO SOUP

Warm up your winter nights with this heartening soup.

SERVES 4-6

50g/2oz butter or margarine
1 large onion, finely chopped
450g/1lb sweet potato, peeled and diced
225g/8oz carrots, peeled and diced
1 tbsp chopped coriander
1 lemon, zest and juice
850ml/1½ pints stock
Pepper

1. Melt the butter or margarine and cook the onion until transparent.

2. Add the sweet potato and carrots and allow to 'sweat' over a very low heat for 10-15 minutes, stirring occasionally.

3. Add the coriander, lemon zest, juice of half the lemon, stock and pepper.

4. Cover and simmer for 30-40 minutes.

5. Liquidise until almost smooth, but leaving some texture to the soup.

6. Return to the pan and reheat until piping hot.

7. Garnish with coriander leaves and serve immediately.

TIME: Preparation takes 15 minutes, cooking takes 40-55 minutes.

SERVING IDEA: Serve with granary rolls.

COOK'S TIP: Fresh coriander may be kept in a jug of water in a cool place. It can also be frozen for use when fresh is not available.

CEE JAY RATATOUILLE

*The ratatouille can be made in advance and
reheated before covering with the apples.*

SERVES 6

1 medium onion, finely sliced
3 cloves garlic, crushed
4 tbsps olive oil
1 large aubergine, diced
1 large red pepper, sliced
2 medium courgettes, sliced
4 medium tomatoes, sliced
1 tsp oregano
Salt and pepper
2 large eating apples, thinly sliced
1oz butter or margarine
Ground cloves

1. Sauté the onion and garlic in the oil until the onion is transparent.

2. Add the aubergine, pepper, courgettes and tomatoes.

3. Cook for a further 5 minutes, stirring occasionally.

4. Add the oregano and seasoning and simmer, covered, for 15-20 minutes.

5. Divide the ratatouille between 6 heated ovenproof dishes and cover each one with a layer of finely sliced apple.

6. Melt the butter or margarine and brush over the top of the apples.

7. Sprinkle with a good pinch of ground cloves and grill until the apples are brown and fluffy.

8. Serve immediately.

TIME: Preparation takes 15 minutes, cooking takes 30 minutes.

COOK'S TIP: This dish will happily keep in a moderate oven for up to 30 minutes.

PAMPLEMOUSSE

A light and easy starter which is simple to prepare.

SERVES 6

3 large grapefruit
3 red skinned apples
4 sticks celery
24 grapes (black or green)
4 tbsps double cream

1. Halve the grapefruit crossways and cut around the inside of the skin to loosen the flesh.

2. Make deep cuts between the segments close to the membranes and remove the segments making sure you do not pierce the skins.

3. Put into a large bowl with any of the juice.

4. Cut away any remaining membranes from the shells with a pair of kitchen scissors, put the grapefruit shells into a plastic bag and store in the refrigerator.

5. Remove the cores from the well washed apples and dice but do not peel.

6. Chop the celery finely.

7. Halve the grapes and remove the seeds.

8. Add the apples, celery and grapes to the grapefruit and stir in the double cream.

9. Refrigerate until required.

10. Just before serving, stir well and pile the mixture into the grapefruit skins.

11. Serve at once.

TIME: Preparation takes 10 minutes.

SERVING IDEA: To make Vandyke grapefruit, snip small V-shapes from the edges of the empty half shells. Serve garnished with fresh mint leaves.

WATERCRESS AND MUSHROOM PÂTÉ

*A delightful pâté which is perfect garnished with lime
or lemon wedges and served with thinly
sliced brown bread and butter.*

SERVES 4

25g/1oz butter
1 medium onion, finely chopped
75g/3oz dark, flat mushrooms, finely
   chopped
1 bunch watercress, finely chopped
100g/4oz low fat curd cheese
Few drops shoyu sauce (Japanese soy
   sauce)
Scant ½ tsp caraway seeds
Black pepper

1. Melt the butter over a low heat and cook the onion until soft but not coloured.

2. Raise the heat, add the mushrooms and cook quickly for 2 minutes.

3. Put in the chopped watercress and stir for about 30 seconds until it becomes limp.

4. Place the contents of the pan in a blender together with the cheese and shoyu sauce.

5. Blend until smooth.

6. Stir in the caraway seeds and pepper to taste.

7. Put into individual ramekin dishes or one large serving dish and chill for at least 2 hours until firm.

TIME: Preparation takes 10 minutes, cooking takes 5 minutes.

COOK'S TIP: It may be necessary to stir the contents of the blender several times as the mixture should be fairly thick.

CRUDITÉS

A great favourite served with delicious dips to accompany.

SERVES 6-8

Choose from the following vegetable selection:

Cauliflower, broccoli - divided into small florets

Carrots, celery, courgettes, cucumber – cut into matchstick pieces

Chicory – separate the blades

Mushrooms – sliced or quartered

Peppers, kohlrabi, fennel – sliced

Radishes, spring onions, cherry tomatoes – leave whole

Tomato and Cheese Dip

1 tbsp butter or margarine

1 tbsp grated onion

225g/8oz tomatoes, peeled and diced

50g/2oz Cheddar cheese, grated

50g/2oz breadcrumbs

1 egg, beaten

½ tsp dried mustard

Salt and pepper

2-4 tbsps Greek yogurt

Creamed Curry Dip

1 tbsp mango chutney

6 tbsps home-made or good quality mayonnaise

1 tsp curry paste

2 tbsp double cream

Pinch ground cumin

Avocado Dip

2 ripe avocados

1 onion, diced

½ clove garlic, crushed

2 tbsps lemon juice

Salt and pepper

Tomato and Cheese Dip

1. Melt the butter and gently fry the onion for 2 or 3 minutes until soft.

2. Add the tomatoes, cover and simmer for 10 minutes.

3. Add the cheese, breadcrumbs and egg and cook for a further minute, stirring all the time, until thickened. Do not allow to boil.

4. Add the mustard and seasoning and blend or liquidise until smooth.

5. Mix in enough Greek yogurt to ensure a smooth 'dipping' consistency and store in the refrigerator until required.

Creamed Curry Dip

1. Chop the pieces of mango with a sharp knife and place in a bowl.

2. Add the other ingredients and mix well.

3. Refrigerate until required.

Avocado Dip

1. Peel the avocados, remove the stones and chop the flesh roughly.

2. Process or liquidise together with the onion, garlic and lemon juice until smooth.

3. Season to taste and refrigerate until required.

TIME: Preparation takes 30 minutes, cooking takes 15 minutes.

FLAGEOLET FIESTA

Serve this dish on its own as a starter or as
a snack with lots of crusty bread.

SERVES 4

225g/8oz flageolet beans, soaked
  overnight
1 medium onion
1 clove garlic
Half a cucumber
2 tbsps chopped parsley
2 tbsps chopped mint
2 tbsps olive oil
Juice and grated rind of 1 lemon
Salt
Freshly ground black pepper
Watercress to garnish

1. Cook the flageolet beans in plenty of boiling water for about 1 hour or until just tender.

2. Drain and put into a mixing bowl.

3. Peel and finely chop the onion.

4. Crush the garlic and chop the cucumber into bite-sized pieces.

5. Add the onion, garlic, cucumber, herbs, oil, lemon juice and rind to the beans and mix well.

6. Add seasoning to taste and leave to marinate for 2 hours.

7. Transfer to a clean serving bowl.

8. Serve garnished with watercress.

TIME: Preparation takes 15 minutes. Marinating takes 2 hours and cooking takes 1 hour.

VARIATION: Substitute red kidney beans for the flageolet beans.

PARSNIP FRITTERS

These tasty fritters make a nice change for lunch or a light snack.

SERVES 4

100g/4oz plain unbleached flour
2 tsps baking powder
1 tsp salt
½ tsp pepper
1 egg
140ml/¼ pint milk
1 tbsp melted butter
680g/1½lbs cooked parsnips, finely
   diced
Oil or clarified butter for frying

1. Sift together the flour, baking powder,
salt and pepper.

2. Beat the egg and mix with the milk and
melted butter.

3. Stir this mixture into the dry
ingredients.

4. Stir in the cooked parsnips.

5. Divide the mixture into 16 and shape
into small fritters.

6. Fry in oil or clarified butter until
browned on both sides.

TIME: Preparation takes 10 minutes, cooking takes about 5-8 minutes per batch.

VARIATION: Courgettes, sweetcorn, onions or aubergine may be
substituted for the parsnips.

SERVING IDEA: Serve with yogurt sauce or make them slightly larger
and serve as a main course with salad.

RED LENTIL SOUFFLÉ

Serve this tasty soufflé as a starter or with watercress or salad for a light lunch.

SERVES 4

100g/4oz red lentils
1 bay leaf
280ml/½ pint water
25g/1oz margarine or butter
75ml/2½ fl.oz double cream
2 egg yolks (size 3)
3 egg whites (size 3)
50g/2oz grated Cheddar cheese (optional)
Salt and pepper
Pinch of paprika

1. Pick over the lentils and remove any stones. Rinse well.

2. Place the lentils, bay leaf and water in a pan and bring to the boil.

3. Simmer for 20 minutes or until the lentils are soft.

4. Remove the bay leaf and beat the lentils until they are very smooth.

5. Beat in the margarine, cream and egg yolks.

6. Beat the egg whites until very stiff and fold into the mixture.

7. Season and fold in the grated cheese.

8. Pour into a well greased souffle dish and sprinkle with a little paprika.

9. Bake in a preheated oven 190°C/375°F/ Gas Mark 5 for approximately 20 minutes or until the souffle is well risen, firm and brown.

10. Serve immediately.

TIME: Preparation takes about 15 minutes, cooking takes 40 minutes.

VARIATION: Add a good pinch of mixed herbs to the lentils whilst cooking.

MIXED NUT BALLS

*This versatile dish can be made in advance and
refrigerated until required for cooking.*
SERVES 8

60g/2½ oz ground almonds
60g/2½ oz ground hazelnuts
60g/2½ oz ground pecan nuts
75g/3oz wholemeal breadcrumbs
100g/4oz Cheddar cheese, grated
1 egg, beaten
4-5 tbsps dry sherry or 2 tbsps milk and 3
   tbsps dry sherry
1 small onion, finely chopped
1 tbsp grated fresh ginger
1 tbsp fresh parsley, chopped
1 small red or green chilli, finely chopped
1 medium red pepper, diced
1 tsp sea salt
1 tsp freshly ground black pepper

1. Mix the almonds, hazelnuts and pecan
nuts together with the breadcrumbs and
the cheese.

2. In another bowl, mix the beaten egg
with the sherry, onion, ginger, parsley,
chilli and red pepper.

3. Combine with the nut mixture and add
the salt and pepper.

4. If the mixture is too dry, add a little
more sherry or milk.

5. Form into small 2cm/1-inch balls.

6. Do not preheat the oven.

7. Arrange the balls on a well greased
baking tray and bake at 180°C/350°F/Gas
Mark 4 for about 20-25 minutes, until
golden brown.

TIME: Preparation takes about 20 minutes, cooking takes 20-25 minutes.

SERVING IDEA: Serve on individual plates on a bed of chopped lettuce. Garnish with slices
of lemon and hand round your favourite sauce in a separate bowl.

HUMMUS

A classic starter which also makes the perfect snack.

SERVES 4

225g/8oz cooked chick peas (reserve stock)
4 tbsps light tahini
Juice of 2 lemons
6 tbsps olive oil
3-4 cloves garlic, crushed
Salt to taste

1. Put the cooked chick peas into a blender together with 140ml/¼ pints of the reserved stock.

2. Add the tahini, lemon juice, half of the olive oil, the garlic, and salt.

3. Blend until smooth, adding a little more stock if it is too thick.

4. Leave to stand for an hour or so to let the flavours develop.

5. Serve on individual dishes with the remaining olive oil drizzled over the top.

TIME: Preparation takes 10 minutes, standing time takes 1 hour.

SERVING IDEA: Serve sprinkled with paprika and garnished with wedges of lemon. Accompany the hummus with warm pitta bread.

BULGAR BOATS

This pretty starter can easily be taken on picnics.

SERVES 6

50g/2oz green lentils
100g/4oz bulgar
1 red pepper
1 green pepper
1 medium onion
50g/2oz pine nuts (dry roasted in a pan)
2 tsps dried salad herbs (tarragon, chives
    or parsley)
Juice and rind of 1 lemon
Salt
Freshly ground black pepper
Cos lettuce to serve

---

1. Remove any grit or stones from the lentils and rinse well.

2. Cover with plenty of water and boil for about 20 minutes - do not overcook.

3. Place the bulgar wheat in a mixing bowl and cover with boiling water. Leave for about 10 minutes - the grain will then have swollen, softened and absorbed the water.

4. Dice the peppers and chop the onion finely.

5. Drain the lentils and add to the wheat, together with the peppers, nuts, onion, herbs, lemon juice and rind, salt and pepper.

6. Using one large lettuce leaf per person, spoon the salad into the centre of the leaves and arrange on a large serving dish garnished with wedges of lemon.

TIME: Preparation takes 15 minutes, cooking takes 20 minutes.

VARIATION: Cashews or peanuts could be used instead of pine nuts. The bulgar mixture could be served in 'parcels' of lightly blanched cabbage leaves.

COOK'S TIP: If the salad is not required immediately, cover and refrigerate until required.

FENNEL AND ORANGE CROUSTADE

A delicious mixture which is simple to prepare.

SERVES 4

4 x 1-inch thick slices wholmeal bread
Oil for deep frying
2 fennel bulbs (reserve any fronds)
4 oranges
1 tbsp olive oil
Pinch salt
Chopped fresh mint for garnishing

1. Trim the crust off the bread and cut into 7.6cm/3-inch squares.

2. Hollow out the middles, leaving evenly shaped cases.

3. Heat the oil and deep fry the bread until golden brown.

4. Drain the bread well on absorbent kitchen paper. Leave to cool.

5. Trim the fennel bulbs and slice thinly. Place in a mixing bowl.

6. Remove all the peel and pith from the oranges and cut into segments - do this over the mixing bowl to catch the juice.

7. Mix the orange segments with the fennel.

8. Add the olive oil and salt and mix together thoroughly.

9. Just before serving, divide the fennel and orange mixture evenly between the bread cases and garnish with fresh mint and fennel fronds.

TIME: Preparation takes 15 minutes, cooking takes 5 minutes.

VARIATION: Serve the salad on individual plates sprinkled with croutons.

COOK'S TIP: The salad can be made in advance and refrigerated until required but do not fill the cases until just before serving.

CARROT AND SWEETCORN MEDLEY

*A delicious combination which is perfect as a
light starter or summer snack.*

SERVES 6

450g/1lb carrots
1 clove garlic, crushed
2-3 tbsps lemon juice
Salt
Freshly ground black pepper
350g/12oz tinned sweetcorn
Lettuce
1 knuckle size piece of fresh root ginger,
    grated
Few black olives, stones removed

1. Scrub and grate the carrots and place in a mixing bowl.

2. Combine the garlic, lemon juice, salt and pepper in a screw topped jar and shake well.

3. Mix the dressing with the grated carrot and add the sweetcorn.

4. Put a little finely shredded lettuce in the bottom of individual stem glasses and arrange the carrot and sweetcorn mixture over the top.

5. Garnish with grated ginger and olives.

6. Chill for 30 minutes before serving.

TIME: Preparation takes 15 minutes, chilling takes 30 minutes.

SERVING IDEA: Serve with wholemeal bread and butter triangles.

VARIATION: To use as an accompaniment to a main course - arrange the carrot on a wide serving plate, leaving an indentation in the centre. Fill this with the sweetcorn and garnish with ginger and olives.

DATE, APPLE AND CELERY STARTER

A healthy dish with a tasty mix of flavours.

SERVES 4

2 dstsp desiccated coconut
2 crisp eating apples
3-4 sticks celery
75g/3oz dates
2 tbsps natural yogurt
Salt and pepper
Pinch of nutmeg

1. Toast the coconut in a dry frying pan over a low heat until it is golden brown, then put to one side.

2. Core and dice the apples and chop the celery finely.

3. Plunge the dates into boiling water, drain and chop finely.

4. Combine the apples, celery and dates in a mixing bowl.

5. Add the yogurt, seasoning and nutmeg and mix thoroughly so that the salad is coated completely.

6. Transfer to a serving bowl and garnish with the toasted coconut.

7. Serve at once.

TIME: Preparation takes 10 minutes, cooking takes 2-3 minutes.

SERVING IDEA: Serve individual portions on a bed of watercress.

COOK'S TIP: Red skinned apples add colour to this salad.

MUSHROOMS AND TOFU IN GARLIC BUTTER

A quick and delicious starter.

SERVES 4

225g/8oz button mushrooms
2.5cm/1" root ginger
225g/8oz smoked tofu
100g/4oz butter
4 small cloves garlic, crushed
2 tbsps chopped parsley

1. Wipe the mushrooms with a damp cloth.

2. Peel and grate the root ringer.

3. Cut the smoked tofu into small 1.2cm./ ½ " squares.

4. Melt the butter in a frying pan.

5. Add the crushed garlic and ginger and fry gently for two minutes.

6. Add the mushrooms and cook gently for 4-5 minutes until the mushrooms are softened.

7. Finally, add the smoked tofu and heat through.

8. Divide between 4 individually heated dishes, sprinkle with chopped parsley and serve at once.

TIME: Preparation takes 10 minutes, cooking takes 12 minutes.

SERVING IDEA: Serve with french bread or crusty wholemeal rolls.

VARIATION: Substitute asparagus tips for the button mushrooms.

SAVOURY TOMATOES

An ideal starter for slimmers.

SERVES 4

4 large Spanish tomatoes
4 tbsps cottage cheese
1 tsp ground cumin
1 green pepper, de-seeded and diced
Seasoning
50g/2oz pumpkin seeds
1 bunch watercress

1. Slice off the tops of the tomatoes.

2. Remove the seeds and leave upside down to drain.

3. Rub the cottage cheese through a sieve to achieve a smooth consistency, add a little milk if necessary.

4. Stir in the cumin, pepper and seasoning.

5. Divide the mixture into four and stuff the tomatoes.

6. Dry roast the pumpkin seeds in a frying pan until they are lightly browned. Sprinkle over the tomatoes.

7. Chill until required.

8. Serve on a bed of watercress.

TIME: Preparation takes 10 minutes.

SERVING IDEA: Serve with very thin slices of brown bread and butter.

VARIATION: Use cream cheese in place of the cottage cheese.

DHINGRI KARI (MUSHROOM CURRY)

An ideal snack or supper dish.

SERVES 4

225g/8oz leeks, finely sliced
2 cloves garlic, crushed
½ tsp grated ginger
2 tsps curry powder
1 tsp garam masala
2 tbsps oil
450g/1lb mushrooms, cut into quarters
100g/4oz creamed coconut, grated
1 tbsp lemon juice

---

1. Fry the leeks, garlic, ginger and spices in the oil until soft.

2. Add the mushrooms and cook over a low heat until soft.

3. Add the grated coconut and cook gently until the coconut has completely dissolved, adding a little water if the mixture appears too dry.

4. Stir in the lemon juice and sufficient salt to taste.

5. Serve on a bed of rice.

TIME: Preparation takes 15 minutes, cooking takes about 20 minutes.

SERVING IDEA: Serve with a tomato and onion salad.

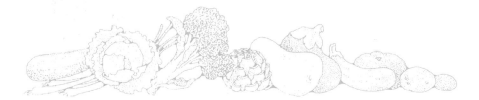

POTATO NESTS

*An ideal supper dish and an excellent
way of using up leftover cooked potatoes.*

SERVES 2

1 onion, finely chopped
450g/1lb potatoes, cooked in their skins
A little milk
Knob of butter
Seasoning
2 eggs
25g/1oz cheese, grated

1. Cook the onion in a little water until softened. Drain.

2. Peel the cooked potatoes and mash them with the milk, butter and seasoning.

3. Add the drained onion and mix well.

4. Divide the mixture into two and make 'nests' on a greased baking sheet.

5. Crack an egg into each nest and sprinkle with grated cheese.

6. Bake at 200°C/400°F/Gas Mark 6 for 20-25 minutes or until the eggs are set.

TIME: Preparation takes 10 minutes, cooking takes 25-30 minutes.

SERVING IDEA: Garnish with parsley and serve with beans and grilled tomatoes or a salad.

VARIATION: The nests may be filled with chopped leftover nut roast mixed with a mushroom or tomato sauce and a few freshly chopped herbs.

POLYGARDOO

*An adaptable dish which can be served
as a snack, side dish or main meal.*

SERVES 4

1 onion, finely chopped
1 clove garlic, crushed
1 tsp bouillon powder dissolved in a little
    boiling water
100g/4oz mushrooms, wiped and sliced
1 small green pepper, chopped
1 x 400g/14oz tin tomatoes, drained
1 pinch of any herb – oregano, sage,
    thyme or mixed herbs
2 x 400g/14oz tin cannellini beans
Salt and pepper
1 tbsp lemon juice
2 tbsps yogurt

1. Cook the onion and garlic with the bouillon powder and water until softened a little.

2. Add the mushrooms and chopped pepper and continue cooking for 3-4 minutes.

3. Add the tomatoes, herbs, beans and seasoning.

4. Mix well and simmer gently for 5 minutes.

5. Remove from the heat and stir in the lemon juice and yogurt.

TIME: Preparation takes 10 minutes, cooking takes 15 minutes.

SERVING IDEA: Serve with pitta bread, rice or pasta for a main meal.

VARIATION: Any type of cooked beans may be used in this dish.

FILO CRACKERS

Serve these delicious snacks anywhere –
buffets, picnics, or drinks parties.

SERVES 4

50g/2oz dried mixed fruit
25g/1oz figs, chopped
50g/2oz ground almonds
50g/2oz dates, chopped
50g/2oz walnuts, chopped
1 tbsp brown sugar
½ tsp ground cinnamon
Zest and juice of 1 orange
25g/1oz melted butter plus 13g/½ oz
    melted butter
16 sheets filo pastry, approximately
    20.3cm x 8" square

1. Put the mixed fruit, figs, ground almonds, dates and walnuts into a mixing bowl.

2. Add the sugar, cinnamon, zest and juice of the orange and the 25g/1oz melted butter. Mix together well and set to one side.

3. Use two sheet together for each cracker. Divide the mixture into 8 and place one portion of the filling in the centre of each sheet.

4. Fold the base of the filo over the filling and roll up.

5. Twist the ends of the filo roll where there is no filling, to form a cracker shape.

6. Place on a greased baking tray and brush generously with the remaining melted butter.

7. Cook at 200°C/400°F/Gas Mark 6 for 20 minutes or until the crackers are golden brown and crisp.

TIME: Preparation takes 20 minutes, cooking takes 20 minutes.

SERVING IDEA: Serve with orange wedges.

COOK'S TIP: Frozen filo pastry may be purchased at most large supermarkets. Allow 2 hours to defrost at room temperature or 3 minutes in a microwave.

WATCHPOINT: A little extra care must be taken when handling filo pastry and it must always be kept well wrapped before use to avoid drying out.

IMAM BAYILDI

Imam Bayildi means "the priest has fainted".
Apparently the dish was so delicious that the
priest fainted with delight!

SERVES 4

2 large aubergines
Salt
150ml/5fl.oz olive oil
2 onions, peeled and finely chopped
2 cloves garlic, crushed
250g/9oz tomatoes, skinned and chopped
½ tsp mixed spice
Juice of ½ lemon
1 tsp brown sugar
1 tbsp chopped parsley
1 tbsp pine kernels
Salt and pepper

1. Halve the aubergines lengthways, and scoop out the flesh with a sharp knife leaving a substantial shell so they do not disintegrate when cooked.

2. Sprinkle the shells with a little salt and leave upside down on a plate for 30 minutes to drain away any bitter juices.

3. Meanwhile, heat half the oil in a saucepan and fry the onion and garlic until just softened.

4. Add the scooped out aubergine flesh, tomatoes, mixed spice, lemon juice, sugar, parsley, pine kernels and a little seasoning.

5. Simmer for about 20 minutes until the mixture has thickened.

6. Wash and dry the aubergine shells and spoon the filling into the halves.

7. Place side by side in a buttered ovenproof dish.

8. Mix the remaining oil with 140ml/¼ pint water and a little seasoning.

9. Pour around the aubergines and bake at 180°C/350°F/Gas Mark 4 for 30-40 minutes or until completely tender.

TIME: Preparation takes 25 minutes, cooking takes 1 hour.

SERVING IDEA: Serve hot or cold garnished with fresh herbs and accompanied by chunks of wholemeal bread. If serving cold, chill for at least 2 hours before serving.

CAULIFLOWER AND BROCCOLI SOUFLETTES

Serve as a winter-time starter or as a main meal with rice salad and ratatouille.

SERVES 6

350g/12oz cauliflower
350g/12oz broccoli
50g/2oz margarine
50g/2oz brown rice flour
420ml/¾ pint milk
50g/2oz Cheddar cheese, grated
1 large egg, separated
Good pinch of nutmeg

1. Break the cauliflower and broccoli into small florets and steam until just tender - about 7-10 minutes.

2. Melt the margarine, remove from the heat and gradually add the flour. Stir to a roux and add the milk gradually, blending well to ensure a smooth consistency.

3. Return the pan to the heat and stir until the sauce thickens and comes to the boil.

4. Cool a little and add the egg yolk and cheese, stir well and add nutmeg to taste.

5. Whip the egg white until stiff and fold carefully into the sauce.

6. Place the vegetables into 6 small buttered ramekin dishes and season.

7. Divide the sauce evenly between the dishes and bake immediately at 190°C/ 375°F/Gas Mark 5 for about 35 minutes until puffed and golden.

8. Serve at once.

TIME: Preparation takes 15 minutes, cooking takes 50 minutes.

SALADS FOR ALL SEASONS

'To remember a successful salad is generally to remember a successful dinner; at all events, the perfect dinner necessarily includes the perfect salad.'

George Ellwanger
Pleasures of the Table 1903

Raw vegetables have always been an important part of our diet and for optimum health it is important that raw food in some form be eaten every day. We are lucky nowadays to find a wide variety of salad ingredients available all year round, although they do tend to be expensive out of season. Today the choice of produce is endless and with organically grown produce you can be sure that the vegetables and the soil have not been treated with chemical sprays or pesticides. Nearly all vegetables are suitable for use in salads, and eaten this way they provide more nutrients than cooked vegetables. Even with careful cooking, valuable vitamins and minerals can be lost.

Vegetables are a valuable source of fibre, vitamins and minerals and, although in most cases they are 80 per cent water, the other 20 per cent contains carbohydrates, fat and protein. To many people, a salad is just a random mix of lettuce, cucumber and tomato. A good salad, however, should be pleasing to the eye as well as the palate. It can be as vibrant as you wish, using red, green, and orange peppers, tomatoes, spring onions, carrots and lettuce, or it can be a tranquil mix of greens using lettuce, cabbage, cucumber, avocado, spring onions and green peppers. The list of ingredients that can be used in salads is as long as your own imagination, so experiment and you will find a salad for every season and every occasion.

GREEK SALAD

*A great favourite which has the added
advantage of being easy to prepare.*

SERVES 4

2 tomatoes
½ green pepper
¼ cucumber
2 sticks celery, finely sliced
1 tsp fresh basil, finely chopped
Few crisp leaves of lettuce
100g/4oz Feta cheese, diced
16 black olives

Dressing
4 tbsps olive oil
2 tbsps lemon juice
1 clove garlic, crushed
Large pinch oregano
Salt and pepper

1. Cut each tomato into eight pieces and
put into a large mixing bowl.

2. Chop the pepper and cucumber
roughly. Add to the tomato together with
the celery and chopped basil.

3. Mix together the oil, lemon juice, garlic,
oregano and seasoning, and pour over the
salad.

4. Mix well to coat all the vegetables.

5. Arrange a few leaves of lettuce in the
bottom of a serving bowl, and pile the
salad on the top, followed by the cheese
cubes.

6. Garnish with olives.

TIME: Preparation takes 15 minutes.

SERVING IDEA: Serve with pitta bread.

VARIATION: Add a few croutons just before serving.

TABOULEH

This is a traditional salad from the Middle East. The main ingredient is bulgar which is partially cooked cracked wheat and only needs soaking for a short while before it is ready to eat.

SERVES 6

175-200g/6-7oz bulgar wheat
1 tsp salt
350ml/12fl.oz boiling water
450g/1lb tomatoes, chopped
½ cucumber, diced
3-4 spring onions

Dressing
50ml/2fl.oz olive oil
50ml/2fl.oz lemon juice
2 tbsps fresh mint
4 tbsps fresh parsley
2 cloves garlic, crushed

1. Mix the bulgar wheat with the salt, pour over the boiling water and leave for 15-20 minutes. All the water will then be absorbed.

2. Mix together the ingredients for the dressing and pour over the soaked bulgar.

3. Fold in lightly with a spoon.

4. Leave for two hours or overnight in a fridge or cool place.

5. Add the salad ingredients and serve.

TIME: Preparation takes about 20 minutes, standing time is about 2 hours.

COOK'S TIP: A few cooked beans can be added to make this dish more substantial.

SERVING IDEA: Serve with flans, cold pies and roasts.

WHEATBERRY SALAD

This makes a substantial salad dish which provides an almost perfect protein balance.

SERVES 4

200g/8oz wheatberries, cooked
100g/4oz kidney beans, cooked
3 medium tomatoes
4 spring onions, chopped
2 sticks celery, chopped
1 tbsp pumpkin seeds

Dressing
4 tbsps olive or sunflower oil
2 tbsps red wine vinegar
1 clove garlic, crushed
1 tsp grated fresh ginger
1 tsp paprika
1 tbsp shoyu (Japanese soy sauce)
Fresh or dried oregano, to taste
Ground black pepper

1. Mix the salad ingredients together, reserving a few pumpkin seeds and spring onions for garnishing.

2. Shake the dressing ingredients together in a screw-topped jar.

3. Pour over the salad and mix gently.

TIME: Preparation takes 20 minutes.

SERVING IDEA: Serve with a lettuce salad.
Wheatberries also mix well with grated carrot and an orange dressing.

COOK'S TIP: This salad keeps well so it can be made in advance and kept in the refrigerator until required.

KENSINGTON SALAD

Decorate the top of this salad with a line of sliced strawberries or kiwi fruit.

SERVES 4-6

3 large mushrooms, thinly sliced
1 medium eating apple, cut into chunks
  and coated with lemon juice
2 celery sticks, cut into matchsticks
25g/1oz walnut pieces
1 bunch watercress

Dressing
1 tbsp mayonnaise
1 tbsp thick yogurt
½ tsp herb mustard
A little lemon juice
Salt and pepper

1. Place the mushrooms, apple, celery and walnuts in a bowl.

2. Combine all the ingredients for the dressing and mix gently with the vegetables.

3. Arrange the watercress on a flat dish or platter and mound the salad mixture on the top.

TIME: Preparation takes about 10 minutes.

VARIATION: A medium bulb of fennel, finely sliced, could be used in place of the celery.

PASTA AND AVOCADO SALAD

The perfect lunch or supper salad for guests.

SERVES 4

225g/8oz pasta shapes
3 tbsps mayonnaise
2 tsps tahini
1 orange
½ medium red pepper, chopped
1 medium avocado
Pumpkin seeds to garnish

1. Cook the pasta until soft and leave to cool.

2. Mix together the mayonnaise and tahini.

3. Segment the orange and chop into small pieces, retain any juice.

4. Chop the pepper.

5. Stir the mayonnaise mixture, pepper and orange (plus juice) into the pasta.

6. Just before serving, cube the avocado and stir in carefully.

7. Serve on an oval dish, decorated with pumpkin seeds.

TIME: Preparation takes 10 minutes, cooking takes about 35 minutes.

WATCHPOINT: Do not peel the avocado until required as it may discolour.

VARIATION: Green pepper may be used in place of the red pepper.

CUCUMBER SALAD

Finely chopped celery may be used in place of fennel in this recipe.

SERVES 6

1 whole cucumber
1 red apple
1 medium-sized fennel, reserve feathery
  leaves for decoration
1 tbsp pine nuts

Dressing
3 tbsps corn oil or sunflower oil
2 tbsps cider vinegar
2 tbsps fresh dill or 1 tsp dried dill
1 tsp caraway seeds
1-2 tsps paprika
Salt and pepper to taste

1. Wash the cucumber but do not peel.
Cut it very thinly and place the slices in a
sieve. Leave to drain for about 20 minutes.

2. Wash and core the apple, slice thinly.

3. Wash and trim the fennel removing the
tough outer leaves and stem. Slice finely.

4. Combine all the ingredients for the
dressing and mix well.

5. Mix with the drained cucumber slices,
apple and fennel.

6. Place the salad in the refrigerator or
keep in a cool place for about an hour
before serving.

TIME: Preparation takes 30 minutes.

SERVING IDEA: Serve decorated with finely chopped fennel leaves
and one tablespoon of pine nuts.

LOLLO ROSSO SALAD

A colourful variation of a Greek Salad.

SERVES 4

½ Lollo Rosso lettuce
3 medium tomatoes, diced
1 red pepper, chopped
1 green pepper, chopped
3 sticks celery, diced
⅓ cucumber, diced
175g/16oz Cheshire cheese
16 black olives

Dressing
1 tbsp tarragon vinegar
3 tbsps olive oil

1. Wash the lettuce and dry it well. Break into pieces with your fingers and put it into a large bowl.

2. Add the tomatoes, pepper, celery, cucumber and cheese.

3. Mix together the vinegar and olive oil, and pour over the salad.

4. Mix gently.

5. Divide the salad between 4 individual dishes and place 4 olives on the top of each one.

TIME: Preparation takes about 10 minutes.

SERVING IDEA: Serve for lunch with crusty rolls or French bread.

VARIATION: If you do not like olives, substitute havled, de-seeded black grapes.

COOK'S TIP: To keep celery crisp, wash well and place the sticks in a jug of cold water in the refrigerator.

RADISH SALAD

Serve this simple salad with a quiche or pie for a light luncheon dish.

SERVES 4

3 bunches radish
1 medium onion
2 large tomatoes
2 tbsps olive oil
2 tbsps lemon juice
Seasoning
1 tbsp chopped parsley

1. Slice the radish and onion finely.

2. Peel and slice the tomatoes.

3. Arrange the vegetables on a serving dish.

4. Put the oil, lemon juice and seasoning into a screw topped jar and shake well.

5. Pour the dressing over the vegetables.

6. Sprinkle with the chopped parsley.

7. Chill before serving.

TIME: Preparation takes 15 minutes. Chilling takes about 30 minutes.

VARIATION: Use red wine vinegar instead of the lemon juice.
Mooli (white radish) can be used in place of the radishes.

MARINATED CARROT SALAD

The perfect light lunch dish or accompaniment to burgers or roasts.

SERVES 4-5

450g/1lb carrots
1 medium onion
1 medium green pepper

Dressing
100ml/4fl.oz tomato juice
100ml/4fl.oz olive oil
100ml/4fl.oz cider vinegar
2 tsps brown sugar
1 level tsp dry mustard power
Seasoning

1. Peel the carrots and cut into matchsticks.

2. Cover with water, bring to the boil and simmer for 4-5 minutes. Drain and allow to cool a little.

3. Slice the onion finely into rings.

4. Cut the pepper into strips.

5. Mix together the dressing ingredients until well blended.

6. Combine the carrots with the onion and pepper and pour the dressing over the top.

7. Marinate overnight, stirring occasionally.

8. Serve garnished with chopped parsley and lemon slices.

TIME: Preparation takes 10 minutes, cooking takes 5 minutes. Marinate overnight.

SERVING IDEA: Serve with cubed cheese and bread to mop up the juices.

VARIATION: If you do not have any tomato juice, use the juice from a tin of tomatoes.

BAVARIAN POTATO SALAD

*It is best to prepare this salad a few hours in advance to
allow the potatoes to absorb the flavours.*

SERVES 4-6

900g/2lbs tiny new potatoes
4 tbsps olive oil
4 spring onions, finely chopped
1 clove garlic, crushed
2 tbsps fresh dill, chopped or 1 tbsp dried
2 tbsps wine vinegar
½ tsp sugar
Seasoning
2 tbsps chopped fresh parsley

1. Wash the potatoes but do not peel, put them into a pan, cover with water and boil until just tender.

2. Whilst the potatoes are cooking, heat the olive oil in a frying pan and cook the spring onions and garlic for 2-3 minutes until they have softened a little.

3. Add the dill and cook gently for a further minute.

4. Add the wine vinegar and sugar, and stir until the sugar melts. Remove from the heat and add a little seasoning.

5. Drain the potatoes and pour the dressing over them whilst they are still hot.

6. Allow to cool and sprinkle with the chopped parsley before serving.

TIME: Preparation takes 15 minutes, cooking takes 15 minutes.

SERVING IDEA: Serve with cold roasts.

CUCUMBER AND PINEAPPLE SALAD

*If you do not have fresh pineapple, use tinned
pineapple without added sugar.*

SERVES 4

2 dstsps raisins
2 tbsps pineapple juice
275g/10oz cucumber
1 red pepper
150g/6oz pineapple
3 tbsps French dressing
1 tsp fresh mint, finely chopped
1 dstsp sesame seeds

1. Soak the raisins in the pineapple juice
for at least half an hour.

2. Slice the cucumber finely.

3. Cut the pepper in half, de-seed, remove
the core and chop finely.

4. Chop the pineapple into cubes.

5. Arrange the cucumber on a serving
dish.

6. Mix the pepper, pineapple and raisins
together and pile in the centre of the
cucumber.

7. Mix the mint into the French dressing
and pour over the salad just before
serving.

8. Sprinkle the sesame seeds over the top.

TIME: Preparation takes 10 minutes, soaking takes 30 minutes.

SERVING IDEA: Serve with flans and roasts.

SPINACH SALAD

Serve with a simple main course.

SERVES 4-6

450g/1lb spinach
1 medium red cabbage
1 medium onion
100g/4oz apricots
6 tbsps French dressing
50g/2oz toasted sunflower seeds

1. Wash the spinach and drain well.

2. First remove the outer leaves and core, then slice the cabbage finely.

3. Slice the onion finely and cut the apricots into slivers.

4. Tear the spinach leaves with the finger into bite-sized pieces and put into a serving dish.

5. Add the sliced cabbage, onion and apricots.

6. Pour over the dressing and mix together thoroughly.

7. Sprinkle with sunflower seeds and serve.

TIME: Preparation takes 15 minutes.

WATCHPOINT: Spinach leaves bruise easily so take care when washing and tearing the leaves.

COOK'S TIP: If using dried apricots, soak beforehand in a little fruit juice.

CARROT AND CELERY SALAD

The addition of quartered hard boiled eggs will make this salad into a very substantial first course.

SERVES 4

225g/8oz carrots
100g/4oz celery
1 red pepper
75g/3oz walnuts
4 tbsps sweetcorn
1 level tsp paprika
¼ tsp chilli powder
4 tbsps French dressing

1. Scrub the carrots and then dice.

2. Slice the celery finely.

3. Remove the core and seeds from the pepper and then dice.

4. Put the carrots, celery and pepper into a serving bowl and add the walnuts and sweetcorn.

5. Mix the paprika and chilli powder into the French dressing and pour over the salad.

6. Mix well and refrigerate for 30 minutes before serving.

TIME: Preparation takes 10 minutes, chilling takes 30 minutes.

SERVING IDEA: Serve as an accompaniment to pasta and grain dishes.

Sunset Salad

Serve this colourful salad with cold nut roasts, raised pies or quiche.

SERVES 4-6

3 dessert apples
350g/¾ lb celery
4 medium mushrooms
75g/3oz walnuts
Lettuce leaves
75g/3oz alfalfa sprouts
75g/3oz black grapes

Dressing
125ml/4fl.oz mayonnaise
50ml/2fl.oz plain yogurt
Seasoning

1. Cut the unpeeled apples into quarters and remove the core. Dice roughly.

2. Dice the celery and slice the mushrooms.

3. Chop the walnuts into quarters.

4. Mix the mayonnaise and yogurt together and season.

5. Put the apples, celery, mushrooms and walnuts into a bowl and fold in the dressing.

6. Line a serving dish with well washed lettuce and spread the sprouts around the outer edge.

7 Pile the salad in the centre and garnish with the grapes.

TIME: Preparation takes 15 minutes.

COOK'S TIP: Use red skinned apples and lettuce tinged with red e.g. Lollo Rosso to give colour to your salad.

102

SEELI SALAD

Serve this very attractive salad for a party or as part of a buffet.

SERVES 4-6

1 large red cabbage
1 green pepper, de-seeded and chopped
½ small pineapple, peeled and finely
  chopped
Segments from 2 medium oranges
6 spring onions, finely chopped
3 sticks celery, chopped
75g/3oz hazelnuts, roughly chopped
75g/3oz sprouted aduki beans

Dressing
100ml/4fl.oz mayonnaise
50ml/2fl.oz Greek yogurt
Seasoning

1. Remove any tough or discoloured outer leaves from the cabbage.

2. Remove the base so that the cabbage will stand upright, and cut about a quarter off the top.

3. Using a sharp knife, scoop out the inside of the cabbage leaving 0.6cm/¼ " for the shell. Set the shell aside.

4. Discard any tough pieces and shred the remaining cabbage very finely.

5. Put the shredded cabbage into a large bowl together with the pepper, pineapple, orange segments, spring onions, celery, hazelnuts and beans.

6. Mix the mayonnaise, yogurt and seasoning together and carefully fold into the vegetables and fruit.

7. Put the mixture into the cabbage shell and place on a serving dish garnished with parsley.

TIME: Preparation takes 20 minutes.

WATCHPOINT: If preparaing in advance, refrigerate the salad and dressing separately and mix them together just before serving.

VARIATION: Walnuts may be used in place of hazelnuts but add them when mixing the salad and dressing together.

GREEN PEPPER SALAD

*Serve in individual dishes as a starter accompanied by
crusty brown bread or as a light lunch with bread and chunks of cheese.*

SERVES 4-6

3 medium green peppers
3 medium tomatoes
2 medium onions
75g/3oz sprouted lentils
Black grapes for garnish
Dressing
4 tbsps olive oil
2 tbsps red wine vinegar
2 tsps cumin
½ tsp fresh coriander, chopped

1. Core and slice the peppers finely.

2. Slice the tomatoes and onions.

3. Arrange the peppers, tomatoes and onions alternately on a round serving dish and sprinkle the lentil sprouts over the top.

4. Mix all the ingredients for the dressing together well and pour over the vegetables.

5. Cover and leave to marinade for at least 1 hour at room temperature before serving.

6. Just before serving, garnish with halved black grapes.

TIME: Preparation takes 10 minutes. Standing time is 1 hour.

COOK'S TIP: You can prepare this salad in advance and refrigerate until required but remove from the refrigerator 30 minutes before serving.

WATCHPOINT: Make sure you only sprout whole lentils, red split lentils will not sprout.

SPROUTED LENTIL SALAD

A quick and easy salad.

SERVES 4-6

225g/8oz broccoli florets
1 red pepper
225g/8oz sprouted lentils
50g/2oz sultanas
4-6 tbsps French dressing
1 tsp freshly grated ginger

1. Cover the broccoli florets with boiling water and leave to stand for 5 minutes. Drain and cool.

2. Core and de-seed the pepper and dice roughly.

3. Arrange the sprouted lentils on a serving dish.

4. Mix together the broccoli florets, pepper and sultanas and pile in the centre.

5. Mix the grated ginger with the French dressing and pour over the salad.

6. Serve at once.

TIME: Preparation takes 15 minutes.

SERVING IDEA: Serve with pastry based dishes.

VARIATION: Cauliflower florets may be used in place of broccoli.

BROCCOLI AND CAULIFLOWER SALAD

Serve this simple salad with crackers.

SERVES 4

1 red pepper
275g/10oz broccoli
275g/10oz cauliflower
1 tbsp roasted almond flakes

Dressing
4 tbsps Greek yogurt
2 tbsps lemon juice
2 tbsps olive oil
Salt and pepper
Pinch of nutmeg

1. De-seed the pepper and cut into matchstick pieces.

2. Wash and trim the broccoli and cauliflower and break into small florets.

3. Place the pepper, broccoli and cauliflower in a mixing bowl.

4. Combine the yogurt, lemon juice, olive oil, seasoning and nutmeg in a screw top jar and shake well.

5. Spoon the dressing over the salad and mix together well.

6. Divide the mixture between 4 individual serving plates and garnish with the almond flakes.

TIME: Preparation takes 10 minutes.

VARIATION: Omit the nutmeg from the dressing and add a few freshly chopped herbs.

SPROUTED ADUKI BEAN SALAD

Serve as an accompaniment to a hot main dish or with cubes
of smoked tofu and lots of crusty French bread for a light luncheon.

SERVES 4

½ cucumber
1 green pepper
225g/8oz aduki beansprouts
75g/3oz toasted peanuts

Dressing
3 tbsps sesame oil
2 tbsps white wine vinegar
1 tbsp shoyu sauce (Japanese soy sauce)
1 tsp brown sugar
Black pepper to taste

1. Chop the cucumber into bite-sized chunks.

2. Cut the pepper in half, de-seed and cut into pieces.

3. Put the cucumber, pepper and beansprouts into a serving dish.

4. Whisk the oil, vinegar, shoyu and sugar together until the sugar has dissolved.

5. Add the pepper to taste.

6. Mix the dressing carefully into the salad and serve at once.

TIME: Preparation takes 10 minutes.

VARIATION: To vary the flavour of the dressing, try walnut oil in place of the sesame oil.

MOUNT CARMEL SALAD

Serve as an accompaniment to a hot main dish.

SERVES 4-6

100g/4oz carrots, peeled
1 green pepper
50g/2oz apricots
1 tbsp sesame seeds
225g/8oz beansprouts
4 tbsps French dressing
2 tbsps pineapple juice

1. Cut the carrots into matchsticks.

2. De-seed and slice the pepper thinly.

3. Cut the apricots into slivers.

4. Toast the seasame seeds in a dry pan over a low heat until they are golden brown and give off a delicious aroma.

5. Place the carrots, pepper, apricots and beansprouts in a serving dish.

6. Mix the French dressing with the pinapple juice and fold into the salad.

7. Sprinkle the sesame seeds over the top.

8. Serve at once.

TIME: Preparation takes 10 minutes.

COOK'S TIP: Use beansprouts which are at least 2.5cm/1" long for this recipe.

LEILA'S SALAD

Serve with stuffed pancakes or simply with crusty
French bread for a light luncheon dish.

SERVES 4-6

275g/10oz long grain brown rice, cooked
225g/8oz prepared pineapple, diced
1 bunch spring onions, finely chopped
50g/2oz flaked almonds, lightly toasted
½ bunch radishes, finely sliced
75g/3oz beansprouts
Twists of lime for garnish

Dressing
3 tbsps sunflower or safflower oil
1 tbsp sherry
Juice of 1 lime
1 tsp grated ginger root
Seasoning

1. Allow the rice to cool.

2. Combine the rice with the pineapple, onions, almonds, radishes and bean sprouts.

3. Mix all the dressing ingredients together.

4. Pour the dressing over the salad and fold in carefully.

5. Refrigerate until required.

6. Garnish with twists of lime.

TIME: Preparation takes 15 minutes, cooking takes 30-35 minutes for the rice.

VARIATION: Use sprouted chickpeas in place of the beansprouts.

SMOKED TOFU SALAD

A tasty main course salad. Serve with granary bread.

SEVES 4-6

225g/8oz broccoli florets
100g/4oz mushrooms
100g/4oz pineapple
4 tbsps sweetcorn
4-6 tbsps French dressing
1 packet smoked tofu, cut into cubes

1. Cover the broccoli florets with boiling water and leave to stand for 5 minutes. Drain and allow to cool.

2. Wipe the mushrooms with a clean cloth and slice thinly.

3. Cut the pineapple into small pieces.

4. Put the broccoli, mushrooms, pineapple and sweetcorn into a large bowl together with the French dressing.

5. Mix carefully.

6. Divide the salad between 4 individual dishes and place the smoked tofu on top.

7. Serve at once.

TIME: Preparation takes 15 minutes.

VARIATION: Omit the tofu and serve as a side salad with savoury flans.

COOK'S TIP: If using plain tofu, marinate for a few hours in equal parts of shoyu sauce and olive oil, together with 1 crushed clove of garlic and 1 tsp of fresh grated ginger.

MAIN MEALS

The main course has traditionally been regarded as the focal point of a meal and the principal source of protein. This is not always the case with a vegetarian meal. For example, pasta alone does not supply enough protein, and nuts or seeds, pulses or some dairy produce needs to be added with the pasta or at some other stage during the meal. If a soup containing lentils or beans, or garnished with grated cheese were followed by a simple pasta dish with a tomato sauce, this would give an adequate supply of protein.

Equally, the same pasta dish followed by a dessert containing milk or eggs would give an equal amount of protein. It's also not always necessary to have one main dish plus two vegetables. Try making smaller portions of one or two main dishes and a couple of starters to give variety and provide an interesting and satisfying meal.

Many of the recipes in this section are easy to make and can be prepared in advance if required. Suggested accompaniments are given, but these are only guidelines, and seasonal vegetables should be used when they are at their cheapest and best. A vegetarian main course is generally much cheaper to produce than a meat meal so you can afford to serve a wide range of dishes or spoil your guests with an exotic dessert.

INDIAN VEGETABLE CURRY

*A wonderfully tasty curry which has the added
advantage of freezing well.*

SERVES 4

Spices
2 tsps turmeric
1 tsp cummin
1 tsp mustard seed
1 tsp fenugreek
4 tsps coriander
½ tsp chilli powder
1 tsp ginger
1 tsp black peppercorns

1lb onions, finely chopped
Ghee or vegetable oil (vary amount to suit
    – about 4 tbsps)
½ pint sterilised milk
2 tbsps white wine vinegar
400g/1 x 14oz tin tomatoes, liquidised
    with their juice
1 tbsp tomato purée
2 tsps brown sugar
1 tsp vegetable bouillon powder or 1
    stock cube dissolved in little boiling
    water
900g/2lbs chopped mushrooms or mixed
vegetables (e.g. mushrooms, cauliflower,
carrots, potatoes, okra)

1. Grind all the spices together, this amount will make 3 tbsps of curry powder.

2. Fry the onions in the ghee or vegetable oil until golden.

3. Add the ground spices, lower the heat and cook for 3 minutes, stirring all the time.

4. Add the milk and vinegar and stir well.

5. Add the liquidised tomatoes, tomato purée, sugar and stock.

6. Bring to the boil, cover and simmer very gently for 1 hour.

7. Add the vegetables and cook until tender – about 30 minutes.

TIME: Preparation takes 30 minutes, cooking takes 1 hour 30 minutes.

SERVING IDEA: Serve with boiled brown rice, chappatis and Cucumber Raita. Cucumber Raita – combine diced cucumber with yogurt, a little chopped mint, a pinch of chilli powder, cumin and seasoning to taste.

FREEZING: The curry sauce will freeze well for up to 3 months so it is well worth while making double the quantity.

LECSO

A popular recipe from Hungary.

SERVES 4-6

---

2 medium green peppers
2 medium yellow peppers
1 large onion, finely sliced
2-3 tbsps sunflower oil
2 tbsps paprika
3 medium tomatoes, skinned and
    quartered
2 eggs, well beaten

---

1. Wash the peppers, core them and cut into strips.

2. Fry the onion in the oil for 1-2 minutes until just coloured.

3. Add the paprika, and stir well.

4. Add the peppers and fry for about 2 minutes.

5. Add the tomatoes and fry for a further minute.

6. Add the beaten eggs and seasoning.

7. Stir well until just cooked.

8. Serve immediately on a bed of rice.

TIME: Preparation takes 10 minutes, cooking takes about 10 minutes.

SERVING IDEA: Lecso can be served with boiled potatoes instead of rice.

VARIATION: Red peppers may be used in place of the yellow peppers.

TOFU BURGERS

*Serve these delicious burgers with mustard and
pickles and accompany with a salad.*

MAKES 8

50g/2oz bulgar wheat
125ml/4fl.oz boiling water
1 small onion, very finely chopped
50g/2oz carrot, grated
50g/2oz mushrooms, very finely chopped
250g/9oz packet tofu
½ tsp basil
½ tsp oregano
2 tbsps shoyu sauce (Japanese soy sauce)
1 tsp tomato purée
Black pepper
Wholewheat flour
Oil for deep frying

---

1. Put the bulgar wheat into a bowl and cover with boiling water. Leave to one side for 15 minutes until all the water has been absorbed.

2. Add the onion, carrot and mushrooms to the bulgar and mix well.

3. Drain the tofu and crumble into the bowl.

4. Add the basil, oregano, shoyu, tomato purée, a little black pepper and 1 tablespoon of wholewheat flour. Mix together well.

5. With wet hands, take heaped tablespoonful of the mixture, squeeze together well and shape into burgers.

6. Coat the burgers with wholewheat flour.

7. Heat the oil until very hot and fry the burgers 3 or 4 at a time until golden brown.

8. Remove and drain on absorbent kitchen paper.

TIME: Preparation takes 15 minutes, cooking takes 5 minutes per batch.

WATCHPOINT: The oil must be very hot otherwise the burgers will disintegrate.

FREEZING: It is well worth while doubling the quantity and freezing a batch of burgers. Freeze for up to 3 months. Reheat by grilling or warming in the oven.

NUTTY POTATO CAKES

This is the perfect way to use up left over potatoes.

MAKES 8 CAKES

450g/1lb potatoes
15g/½ oz margarine or butter
A little milk
75g/3oz mixed nuts, finely ground
25g/1oz sunflower seeds, finely ground
2 tbsps spring onions, finely chopped
Freshly ground black pepper
Wholemeal flour for coating
Oil for frying

1. Peel the potatoes, cut into pieces and boil until just soft.

2. Drain and mash with the butter and milk to a creamy consistency.

3. Add the nuts, seeds, onions and pepper to taste.

4. If necessary, add a little more milk at this stage to give a soft texture which holds together.

5. Form into 8 cakes.

6. Coat with flour and fry quickly in as little oil as possible.

7. Drain on kitchen roll.

8. Serve hot.

TIME: Preparation takes 10 minutes, cooking takes 25 minutes.

SERVING IDEA: Serve with a green salad and sliced tomatoes in an oil and fresh basil dressing.

VARIATION: Dry roast the sunflower seeds until golden brown, before grinding.

STUFFED MARROW

This makes a nice change from the more common stuffed vegetables.

SERVES 4

1 medium marrow
6 tbsps fresh brown breadcrumbs
2-4 tbsps milk
4 eggs, hard boiled
100g/4oz grated cheese
Salt and pepper
Pinch of freshly grated nutmeg
1 egg, beaten
A little margarine or butter
Parsley and 1 red pepper for garnish

1. Wash the marrow well, cut in half lengthwise and scoop out the seeds.

2. Place in a well greased baking tin or dish.

3. Soak the breadcrumbs in the milk.

4. Chop the hard-boiled eggs and add to the breadcrumbs together with the cheese, seasoning and nutmeg.

5. Bind the mixture with the beaten egg.

6. Pile into the marrow halves and dot with knobs of margarine or butter.

7. Pour a little water around the marrow and bake in a moderate oven, 190°C/375°F/Gas Mark 5 for 35-40 minutes until the marrow is tender and the top is nicely browned. (If the top is browning too quickly, cover with greaseproof paper.)

8. Serve on a large dish garnished with parsley and red pepper rings.

TIME: Preparation takes 25 minutes, cooking takes 35-40 minutes.

SERVING IDEA: For a special occasion garnish with cranberries and surround with sliced red or yellow peppers, chopped lettuce and watercress.

COOK'S TIP: If the marrow is old it may be better to partly bake the shell before adding the filling.

STUFFED COURGETTES

*Serve as a starter or accompany with a parsley
sauce and potatoes for a light lunch.*

SERVES 4

4 medium courgettes
2 tbsps olive oil
1 onion, very finely chopped
100g/4oz carrots, grated
½ tsp paprika
1 tsp cumin seeds
¼ tsp turmeric
¼ tsp asafetida powder (optional)
100g/4oz creamed coconut, grated

1. Wash the courgettes and cut in half lengthwise.

2. Using a teaspoon, remove the flesh leaving about 0.6cm/¼ " shell.

3. Chop the flesh finely.

4. Heat the oil and sauté the onion for a few minutes.

5. Add the carrots, courgette flesh and spices and cook, stirring frequently, for a further 5 minutes until softened.

6. Remove from the heat and stir in the creamed coconut.

7. Divide the mixture between the courgette shells making sure that it covers the exposed part of the flesh.

8. Place the courgettes in a greased ovenproof casserole and cook at 190°C/375°F/Gas Mark 5 for 45 minutes until the courgette shells are soft.

9. Serve immediately.

TIME: Preparation takes 10 minutes, cooking takes 55 minutes.

COOK'S TIP: Creamed coconut can be bought at delicatessens, health food shops and most supermarkets. Asafetida powder is available from Indian shops.

TASTY TOMATO SAUCE

*Serve this adaptable sauce over stuffed
aubergines, marrow or peppers.*

SERVES 4

25g/1oz pine kernels
Pinch of salt
1 tsp sunflower oil
1 onion, peeled and chopped
Pinch of chilli powder
3 cloves
400g/1 x 14oz tin tomatoes

1. Place the pine kernels in a frying pan and dry roast. Remove when they are lightly browned and sprinkle with the salt.

2. Fry the onion in the sunflower oil until soft.

3. Add the chilli powder and cloves. Fry for 1 minute.

4. Add the tomatoes, bring to the boil and simmer for 10 minutes.

5. Cool slightly and remove the cloves.

6. Blend the mixture in a liquidiser and return to pan. Add the pine kernels and gently reheat.

TIME: Preparation takes 10 minutes, cooking takes 15 minutes.

WATCHPOINT: Dry roast the pine kernels over a low heat, stirring continuously, otherwise they will burn.

BUTTER BEAN ROAST

*A combination of simple ingredients makes this
a useful recipe for mid-week meals.*

SERVES 4

225g/8oz dried butter beans
2 large onions
A little oil for frying
175g/6oz mushrooms, sliced
100g/4oz cooked rice
1 egg, beaten
1 tbsp freshly chopped parsley
1 tsp dried mixed herbs
Salt and pepper

---

1. Soak the beans overnight, change the water and cook until soft – about 1-1¼ hours.

2. Drain and mash the beans thoroughly.

3. Slice the onions finely and fry in a little oil until golden brown, adding the mushrooms after 10 minutes.

4. Mix all the ingredients together in a bowl.

5. Place the mixture in a greased 450g/1lb loaf tin and bake at 190°C/375°F/Gas Mark 5 for 30 minutes or until browned on top.

TIME: Preparation takes 10-15 minutes, bean cooking takes 1-1¼ hours, and cooking takes 30 minutes for roast.

SERVING IDEA: Serve with potatoes and salad.

FREEZING: Prepare to the end of Step 4. Place the mixture in the loaf tin, cover with foil and freeze for up to 2 months. To de-frost, remove from freezer 8 hours before required and allow to defrost at room temperature. Cook as above.

PERFECT POTATOES

*Potatoes become extra special when teamed
up with the flavour of onion.*

SERVES 5

900g/2lbs potatoes
1 large onion
Salt and pepper
280ml/½ pint milk
40g/1½ oz butter or margarine

1. Peel and finely slice the potatoes and onion.

2. Layer the potato slices and onion in a shallow ovenproof dish, sprinkling each layer with some salt and pepper.

3. Pour over the milk and dot with the butter or margarine.

4. Bake uncovered in a preheated oven, 180°C/350°F/Gas Mark 4 for 1-1½ hours or until the potatoes are soft, golden and brown on top.

TIME: Preparation takes 15 minutes, cooking takes 1-1½ hours.

SERVING IDEA: Serve with grilled mushrooms and tomatoes for a supper dish or serve with roasts, burgers or pies.

FREEZING: Cook quickly, cover with foil and place in a freezer bag. Thaw at room temperature for 4-6 hours and reheat at 190°C/375°F/Gas mark 5 for about 30 minutes.

VARIATION: Place a layer of finely sliced cooking apples in the bottom of the dish.

VALENCIA LOAF

This loaf is delicious served with an apple sauce and a variety of vegetables.

SERVES 6

2 large onions
75ml/3fl.oz oil
75g/3oz spaghetti
50g/2oz brown breadcrumbs
225g/8oz ground almonds
2 eggs, beaten
1 tsp sage
Rind and juice of 1 lemon
Salt and pepper

1. Peel and slice the onions and fry in the oil for 10 minutes over a low heat.

2. Cook the spaghetti in boiling, salted water until *al dente*.

3. Drain the spaghetti and add the onion, breadcrumbs, almonds, eggs, sage, lemon juice and rind. Season to taste.

4. Stir carefully and put into a lined and greased 900g/2lb loaf tin.

5. Cover and bake in a moderate oven 190°C/375°F/Gas mark 5 for 1 hour.

6. Turn out onto a serving dish and remove the lining paper carefully.

7. Cut into thick slices and serve immediately.

TIME: Preparation takes 15 minutes, cooking takes 1 hour 20 minutes.

VARIATION: 50g/2oz of soya flour mixed with a little water may be used in place of the eggs.

DEEP MUSHROOM PIE

*A delicious pie and so adaptable. Serve with
salad or potatoes and a green vegetable.*

SERVES 4

Filling
1 tbsp vegetable oil
350g/¾ lb mushrooms, cleaned and
    chopped
225g/8oz mixed nuts, finely milled
2 medium onions, peeled and finely
    chopped
100g/4oz wholewheat breadcrumbs
2 eggs, beaten
1 tsp dried thyme or 2 tsps fresh
1 tsp dried marjoram or 2 tsps fresh
1 tbsps shoyu (Japanese soy sauce)
Salt and pepper to taste
Small quantity of stock to achieve right
    consistency if necessary

Pastry
350g/12oz wholewheat flour
Pinch of salt
1 tsp baking powder (optional)
100g/4oz solid vegetable fat
100ml/4fl.oz water plus extra boiling
    water as necessary
Beaten egg to glaze

1. Heat the oil in a large saucepan and
gently fry the onion until soft.

2. Add the finely chopped mushrooms
and cook until the juices begin to run.

3. Remove from the heat and add all the
other filling ingredients to form a thick,
but not dry, consistency adding a little
stock or water if necessary. Allow to cool.

4. To prepare the pastry, first sift the
flour, salt and baking powder into a large
mixing bowl.

5. Cut the fat into small pieces and melt in
a saucepan. Add the cold water and bring
to a fierce, bubbling boil.

6. Immediately pour into the centre of the
flour and mix vigorously with a wooden
spoon until glossy.

7. When the mixture is cool enough to
handle, use hands and knead it into a ball.

8. Divide the mixture into two-thirds and
one-third, placing the one-thirds portion in
an oiled plastic bag to prevent drying out.

9. Use the two-thirds portion to line the
base and sides of a 19cm/7" spring mould,
pressing it down and moulding it into
position.

10. Spoon in the mushroom filling, press
down firmly making a "dome" shape.

11. Roll out the remaining pastry to just
larger than the tin and place on top of the
pie, pinching the edges together to seal.

12. Trim off excess pastry and glaze
generously with beaten egg.

13. Cut or prick vents in the lid to allow
the steam to escape.

14. Bake at 220°C/425°F/Gas Mark 7 for
20 minutes. Reduce to 190°C/375°F/Gas
Mark 5 and bake for a further hour.

15. Unmould and serve on an attractive
platter surrounded by watercress and
twists of lemon and cucumber.

TIME: Preparation takes about 35 minutes,
    cooking takes 1 hour 20 minutes.

SPINACH, CORN AND NUT RAISED PIE

An attractive pie which is suitable for family meals and entertaining.

SERVES 6

450g/1lb spinach
1 onion, chopped
2 tbsps oil
100g/4oz hazelnuts, finely chopped
100g/4oz brazil nuts, finely chopped
100g/4oz wholemeal breadcrumbs
100g/4oz sweetcorn
1 tsp oregano
½ tsp sage
1 tbsp freshly chopped parsley
1 tsp shoyu (Japanese soy sauce)
2 tbsps tahini
280ml/½ pint stock
Salt and pepper

Pastry
325g/12oz wholemeal flour
1 tsp baking powder
100g/4oz vegetable fat
175ml/6fl.oz water
Pinch of salt

1. Steam the spinach until soft. Drain well and chop finely.

2. Fry the onion in the oil until soft.

3. Mix together all the dry ingredients, add the shoyu, tahini and sufficient stock to give a moist texture.

4. Season to taste.

5. For the pastry, mix together the dry ingredients.

6. Melt the fat in the water and heat until about to boil.

7. Add the liquid to the flour and mix well. Add extra boiling water if the mixture is too dry.

8. Put two thirds of the dough into a 17.8cm/7" pie tin and push into shape.

9. Put the filling into the pie case and press down well.

10. Roll out the remaining dough and make a pie lid.

11. Glaze the top and make two small steam holes.

12. Bake at 210°C/425°F/Gas mark 7 for 20 minutes, reduce the heat to 190°C/375°F/Gas Mark 5 for a further 50 minutes or until golden brown.

TIME: Preparation takes about 40 minutes, cooking takes about 1 hour 15 minutes.

SERVING IDEA: Serve hot with vegetables or cold with salad.

COOK'S TIP: There is no need to grease the pie tin when using hot water pastry.

SWEETCORN AND PARSNIP FLAN

Serve this unusual flan with jacket potatoes
filled with cottage cheese and chives.

SERVES 6

Base
75g/3oz soft margarine
175g/6oz wholemeal flour
1 tsp baking powder
Pinch of salt
4-6 tbsps ice-cold water
1 tbsp oil

Filling
1 large onion, peeled and finely chopped
1 clove garlic, crushed
25g/1oz butter or margarine
2 large parsnips, steamed and roughly
    mashed
175g/6oz sweetcorn, frozen or tinned
1 tsp dried basil
Salt and pepper
3 eggs
140ml/¼ pint milk
75g/3oz grated Cheddar cheese
1 medium tomato, sliced

1. Rub the margarine into the flour, baking powder and salt until the mixture resembles fine breadcrumbs.

2. Add the water and oil and work together lightly. The mixture should be fairly moist.

3. Leave for half an hour.

4. Roll out and line a 25.4cm/10" flan dish.

5. Prick the bottom and bake blind at 210°C/425°F/Gas Mark 7 for about 8 minutes.

6. Meanwhile, sauté the onion and garlic in the butter or margarine until soft and golden.

7. Add the parsnips, sweetcorn and basil and season to taste.

8. Beat the eggs and add the milk.

9. Add to the vegetable mixture and stir over a low heat until the mixture just begins to set.

10. Pour into the flan base and top with the grated cheese and sliced tomato.

11. Bake 190°C/375°F/Gas Mark 5 for 15-20 minutes or until the cheese is golden brown.

TIME: Preparation takes about 40 minutes, cooking takes 30 minutes.

COOK'S TIP: The partial cooking of the whole mixture before placing in the flan base helps to keep the base from becoming soggy and considerably reduces the cooking time.

RATATOUILLE PIE WITH CHEESE AND PEANUT PASTRY

*A colourful dish to make in the autumn when aubergines
and courgettes are cheap and plentiful.*

SERVES 4-6

Ratatouille
2 tbsps olive oil
2 onions, chopped
4 tomatoes, sliced
1 aubergine, sliced
3 courgettes, finely sliced
2 sticks celery, chopped

White sauce
50g/2oz flour
50g/2oz margarine
430ml/¾ pint milk

Pastry
50g/2oz butter
100g/4oz self raising flour
50g/2oz finely grated cheese
50g/2oz finely chopped salted peanuts
A little milk
Beaten egg

1. Put the oil and all the vegetables into a large pan and cook gently for about 20 minutes or until soft.

2. To make the sauce, melt the margarine in a separate pan, stir in the flour and cook for 2 minutes, stirring all the time.

3. Gradually add the milk and bring to boiling point.

4. Stir the sauce into the vegetable mixture and put into an ovenproof dish.

5. Rub the butter into the flour and add the cheese and peanuts.

6. Add a little milk and roll out the pastry.

7. Place on top of the ratatouille mixture, trim and brush with beaten egg.

8. Bake 190°C/375°F/Gas Mark 5 for about 30 minutes or until golden brown.

TIME: Preparation takes 30 minutes, cooking takes 1 hour.

SERVING IDEA: Serve with bundles of julienne vegetables – carrots, swede, turnips etc.

VARIATION: Sliced green pepper can be used in place of the celery.

SWEET POTATO AND FRENCH BEAN PASTIES

These pasties are a tasty addition to any lunch box or picnic basket.

SERVES 4

225g/8oz wholemeal shortcrust pastry
½ medium onion, finely chopped
1 clove garlic, crushed
1 tbsp oil
½ tsp freshly grated ginger
¼ – ½ tsp chilli powder
¼ tsp turmeric
½ tsp ground cumin
1 tsp ground coriander
¼ tsp mustard powder
1 medium-sized sweet potato, cooked and
    finely diced
100g/4oz French beans, chopped into
    1.2cm/½" lengths
2 tbsps water or stock
Salt and pepper

1. Fry the onion and garlic in the oil until soft.

2. Add the ginger and all the spices and stir.

3. Add the diced potato, beans and water or stock and cook gently for 4-5 minutes or until the beans begin to cook.

4. Allow the mixture to cool and season well.

5. Roll out the pastry into 4 circles.

6. Place a quarter of the filling in the centre of each circle and dampen the edges of the pastry with a little water.

7. Join the pastry together over the filling.

8. Make a small hole in each pasty and glaze with milk or egg.

9. Bake for 15-20 minutes at 200°C/400°F/ Gas Mark 6.

TIME: Preparation, including making the pastry, takes 25 minutes.
Cooking takes 15-20 minutes.

FREEZING: The pasties will freeze well for up to 2 months. Thaw at room temperature.

153

NUTTY SPAGHETTI

An easy-to-make lunch or supper dish.

SERVES 4

225g/8oz spaghetti
710ml/1¼ pints boiling, salted water
1 onion, finely chopped
2 tbsps sunflower oil
2½ tsps curry powder
175ml/6fl.oz tomato juice
3 tbsps crunchy peanut butter
1 tbsp lemon juice
Lemon twists and peanuts for garnish

1. Boil the spaghetti until just tender and drain well.

2. Fry the onion in the oil until golden brown.

3. Stir in the curry powder, tomato juice, peanut butter and lemon juice.

4. Simmer for 5 minutes and then stir into the spaghetti.

TIME: Preparation takes about 10 minutes, cooking takes 25 minutes.

SERVING IDEA: Serve garnished with lemon twists and peanuts.

VARIATION: Almond butter and blanched almonds can be used in place of the peanut butter and peanuts.

CONCHIGLIE WITH TWO SAUCES

A very low fat pasta dish with two delicious sauces.

SERVES 4

450g/1lb cooked conchiglie (pasta shells)

Tomato sauce
1 large onion, very finely chopped
1 tsp bouillon powder
3 tbsps water
1 clove garlic, crushed
½ tsp dried thyme
Pinch ground rosemary
400g/1 x 14oz tin tomatoes

Mushroom sauce
250g/9oz oyster mushrooms
25g/1oz low fat margarine
1 tsp bouillon powder
4 tbsps fromage frais
Chopped parsley for garnish

---

1. To make the tomato sauce, place the onion, bouillon powder, water and garlic in a pan and cook very gently for 7-10 minutes until the onion is soft.

2. Add the thyme and rosemary and cook for 1 minute.

3. Chop the tinned tomatoes and add to the pan together with the tomato juice.

4. Bring to the boil and boil rapidly until the sauce has reduced and thickened.

5. To make the mushroom sauce, chop the mushrooms finely.

6. Melt the margarine in a pan and add the bouillon powder and mushrooms.

7. Simmer very gently for 10-15 minutes.

8. Remove from the heat and stir in the fromage frais.

9. Heat gently until hot but do not boil.

10. Divide the pasta between 4 serving dishes and pour the tomato sauce over one half of the pasta and the mushroom sauce over the other side of the pasta.

11. Sprinkle the chopped parsley between the two sauces.

12. Serve at once.

TIME: Preparation takes 20 minutes, cooking, including the pasta, takes 35 minutes.

COOK'S TIP: The sauces may be prepared in advance, refrigerated and reheated when required.

VARIATION: Fresh pasta is nicest but any pasta can be used and both sauces are suitable for use on their own – just double the quantities given.

COURGETTE AND CARROT LAYER

*Serve with a sprouted salad for a light lunch or glaze
with agar and fresh herbs for a special occasion.*

SERVES 4

450g/1lb carrots, cooked, mashed and
    seasoned
1 medium onion
450g/1lb courgettes, finely chopped
1 tbsp oil
100g/4oz almonds, finely chopped or
    ground
75g/3oz wholemeal breadcrumbs
1 tsp Vecon (vegetable stock) dissolved in
    a little boiling water
1 egg beaten
1 level tsp mixed herbs
1 tbsp tomato purée
1 tbsps shoyu sauce (Japanese soy sauce)
Ground black pepper

1. Grease and line a 450g/1lb loaf tin.

2. Fry the onion and courgettes in the oil,
add all the remaining ingredients except
the carrot, and mix together well.

3. Place half of the courgette mixture into
the loaf tin and press down well.

4. Arrange the carrots on top of this
followed by the remaining courgette
mixture.

5. Cover with foil and cook for 1 hour at
175°C/350°F/Gas Mark 4.

6. Allow to cool for 10 minutes before
removing from tin.

TIME: Preparation, including cooking the carrots, takes 25 minutes.

COOK'S TIP: This mixture makes a delicious filling for a raised pie.

COURGETTE AND SWEETCORN SAVOURY

This is an excellent way to use up leftover pasta.

SERVES 4

1 tbsp oil
1 medium onion, chopped
225g/8oz courgettes, sliced
200g/7oz tin sweetcorn, drained
175g/6oz cooked pasta shapes
Large pinch oregano
1 tbsp tomato purée
Salt and pepper

Sauce
25g/1oz margarine
25g/1oz wholewheat flour
275ml/½ pint skimmed milk
3 tbsps white wine
50g/2oz strong cheese, grated

Topping
25g/1oz wholemeal breadcrumbs
1 dstsp sunflower seeds

1. Heat the oil in a frying pan and sauté the chopped onion until soft.

2. Add the sliced courgettes and brown lightly.

3. Mix in the sweetcorn, cooked pasta, oregano and tomato purée, and stir.

4. Season lightly and transfer the mixture to an oiled ovenproof dish.

5. Make the cheese sauce by melting the margarine and stirring in the flour to make a roux. Cook gently for a few minutes and then pour on the milk and wine, stirring all the time, to make a smooth sauce.

6. Add the grated cheese and stir until it melts into the sauce. Remove from the heat and pour over the vegetable mixture.

7. Top with the breadcrumbs and sunflower seeds.

8. Bake 180°C/350°F/Gas Mark 4 for about 20 minutes until the dish is brown and bubbling.

TIME: Preparation takes about 30 minutes, cooking takes 20 minutes.

SERVING IDEA: Serve with grilled tomatoes and creamed potatoes.

Winter Crumble

*A variety of hearty vegetables topped with oats and
cheese makes the perfect winter meal.*

SERVES 4-6

Topping
75g/3oz butter or margarine
100g/4oz wholewheat flour
50g/2oz rolled oats
100g/4oz Cheddar cheese, grated
¼ tsp salt

175ml/6fl.oz stock or water
280ml/½ pint sweet cider
1 tsp brown sugar
2 carrots, chopped
2 large parsnips, cut into rings
2 sticks celery, chopped
2 heads broccoli, cut into florets
¼ cauliflower, cut into florets
1 dstsp wholewheat flour
2 tbsps chopped parsley
1 medium onion, chopped and fried until
   golden
4 large tomatoes, peeled and sliced
225g/8oz cooked black-eyed beans
Salt and pepper

1. Make the topping by rubbing the butter
into the flour and oats until the mixture
resembles fine breadcrumbs.

2. Stir in the cheese and salt.

3. Mix the stock with the cider and sugar
and put into a large pan with the carrots
and parsnips.

4. Cook until just tender, remove the
vegetables and put aside.

5. Add the celery, broccoli and cauliflower
to the pan, cook until tender, remove and
reserve with other vegetables.

6. Mix the flour with a little water, add to
the cider and cook until thickened, stirring
all the time.

7. Cook for 2-3 minutes, remove from the
heat and add the parsley.

8. Place the onions, vegetables, tomatoes
and beans in a greased casserole and
season well. Pour the sauce over the
mixture.

9. Sprinkle the topping over the top and
press down a little.

10. Cook at 200°C/400°F/Gas mark 6 for
30-35 minutes or until the topping is
golden brown.

TIME: Preparation takes 20 minutes, cooking takes 1 hour 5 minutes.

SERVING IDEA: Serve with roast potatoes.

COOK'S TIP: The casserole can be prepared in advance to the end of Step 9.
Refrigerate until ready to cook.

RATATOUILLE LASAGNE

Serve with crusty rolls and a green salad
for the perfect lunch or supper.

SERVES 4-6

6 strips lasagne verdi or wholemeal
  lasagne
2-3 tbsps olive oil
2 onions, finely chopped
2 cloves garlic, crushed
1 large aubergine, chopped
1 courgette, sliced thinly
1 green pepper, chopped
1 red pepper, chopped
400g/1 x 14oz tin tomatoes, chopped
2-3 tbsps tomato purée
A little vegetable stock
Salt and freshly ground black pepper

White sauce
25g/1oz butter or margarine
25g/1oz wholemeal flour
280ml/½ pint milk

40g/1½ oz Parmesan cheese, grated
Parsley, to garnish

1. Preheat the oven to 180°C/350°F/Gas
Mark 4.

2. Cook the lasagne in boiling, salted
water for 12-15 minutes.

3. Plunge into a bowl of cold water to
prevent overcooking or sticking.

4. Heat the oil and fry the onion and
garlic until soft.

5. Add the aubergine, courgette and
peppers and sauté until soft.

6. Add the tomatoes with their juice and
the tomato purée and simmer until tender.
It may be necessary to add a little stock at
this stage.

7. Season well and set aside.

8. Make the white sauce by melting the
butter in a small saucepan.

9. Add the flour and cook to a roux.

10. Add the milk slowly, stirring
constantly, bring to the boil and simmer
for about 5 minutes. Remove from the
heat.

11. Grease a deep ovenproof dish.

12. Layer the ratatouille and lasagne strips,
starting with the ratatouille and finishing
with a layer of lasagne.

13. Pour over the white sauce and
sprinkle the Parmesan cheese over the
top.

14. Bake in the oven for 35 minutes until
golden. Garnish with parsley before
serving.

TIME: Preparation takes about 20 minutes, cooking takes 1 hour.

VARIATION: If aubergine is not available, 225g/8oz sliced mushrooms may be used instead.

SAVOURY BEAN POT

Serve this exciting mixture with rice or jacket potatoes and a salad.

SERVES 4

2 tbsps vegetable oil
2 vegetable stock cubes, crumbled
2 medium onions, chopped
2 eating apples, peeled and grated
2 medium carrots, grated
3 tbsps tomato purée
280ml/½ pint water
2 tbsps white wine vinegar
1 tbsp dried mustard
1 level tsp oregano
1 level tsp cumin
1 dstsp brown sugar
Salt and pepper
450g/1lb cooked red kidney beans
A little soured cream

1. Heat the oil in a non-stick pan.

2. Add the crumbled stock cubes, onions, apples and carrots.

3. Sauté for 5 minutes, stirring continuously.

4. Mix the tomato purée with the water and add together with all the other ingredients apart from the beans and cream.

5. Stir well, cover and simmer for 2 minutes.

6. Add the beans and tip the mixture into an ovenproof casserole.

7. Cover and cook at 180°C/350°F/Gas Mark 4 for 35-40 minutes.

8. Add a little more water after 20 minutes if necessary.

9. Top with swirls of soured cream and serve.

TIME: Preparation takes 20 minutes, cooking takes 45 minutes.

VARIATION: Use cider vinegar in place of the white wine vinegar.

VEGETABLE STEW WITH HERB DUMPLINGS

The ideal meal to warm up a cold winter's night.

SERVE 4-6

1 large onion
900g/2lbs mixed vegetables (carrot,
    swede, parsnips, turnips,
    cauliflower etc.)
570ml/1 pint stock or water plus a
    stock cube
Salt and pepper
Flour or proprietory gravy powder to
    thicken

Dumplings
100g/4oz wholewheat self-raising flour
50g/2oz vegetarian suet
1 tsp mixed herbs
¼ tsp salt

1. Chop the onion into large pieces.

2. Peel and prepare the vegetables and chop into bite-sized pieces.

3. Put the onion and vegetables into a pan and cover with the stock.

4. Bring to the boil and simmer for 20 minutes.

5. Season to taste.

6. Mix a little flour or gravy powder with a little water and stir into the stew to thicken.

7. Place the ingredients for the dumplings into a bowl and add just enough water to bind.

8. Shape the mixture into 8 small dumplings.

9. Bring the stew to the boil and drop in the dumplings.

10. Cover and allow to simmer for 10 minutes.

11. Serve at once.

TIME: Preparation takes 10 minutes, cooking takes 30 minutes.

SERVING IDEA: Serve with boiled potatoes.

VARIATION: The mixed herbs may be omitted when making the dumplings or chopped fresh parsley and a squeeze of lemon juice may be used instead.

MUSHROOM STROGANOFF

A great favourite which is much appreciated by all age groups.

SERVES 4-6

2 medium onions, sliced
5 sticks celery, chopped
50g/2oz butter or margarine
450g/1lb tiny button mushrooms
½ tsp mixed herbs
½ tsp basil
1 large heaped tbsp unbleached flour
280ml/½ pint stock
Salt and pepper
65ml/2½ fl.oz soured cream or yogurt
Chopped parsley

1. Put the onions and celery into a large pan together with the butter or margarine and sauté over a low heat until the onions are transparent.

2. Add the mushrooms and cook for 2-3 minutes until the juices run.

3. Add the mixed herbs and basil.

4. Stir in the flour and cook for 1 minute.

5. Add the stock and seasoning and allow to cook gently for 8-10 minutes.

6. Remove from the heat, stir in the soured cream and adjust the seasoning if necessary.

7. Heat very gently to serving temperature but do not allow to boil.

8. Garnish with the chopped parsley and serve at once.

TIME: Preparation takes 10 minutes, cooking takes 20 minutes.

SERVING IDEA: Serve on a bed of Walnut Rice – cook enough rice to serve 4-6 people and carefully fold in seasoning, a little butter, 1 crushed clove of garlic and 50g/2oz finely chopped walnuts.

COOK'S TIP: If tiny button mushrooms are not available use the larger variety and slice thickly.

FIFTEEN MINUTE GOULASH

This quick and easy goulash is best served with baked potatoes.

SERVES 4

1 onion, finely chopped
1 clove garlic, crushed
2 carrots, diced
3 medium courgettes, diced
2 tbsps olive oil
1 tbsp paprika
Pinch of nutmeg
1 heaped tsbp freshly chopped parsley
1 tbsp tomato purée
1 x 400g/14oz tin tomatoes
225g/8oz cooked red kidney beans or 1 x
    14oz tin, drained and washed
225g/8oz cooked white kidney beans or 1
    x 14oz tin, drained and washed
140ml/¼ pint tomato juice or stock
Salt and pepper
Soured cream or yogurt to serve

1. Put the onion, garlic, carrots and courgettes into a pan with the olive oil and sauté for 5 minutes until softened.

2. Stir in the paprika, nutmeg, parsley and tomato purée.

3. Add the rest of the ingredients except cream or yogurt and cook over a low heat for 10 minutes.

4. Turn onto a hot serving dish and top with a little soured cream or yogurt.

TIME: Preparation takes 10 minutes, cooking takes 15 minutes.

VARIATION: Vary the type of bean used – try haricots, soya beans or even chick peas.

Scone Based Pizza

A bumper sized pizza for four hungry people.

SERVES 4-6

Base
90g/3½ oz margarine
200g/7oz wholemeal flour
2 small eggs plus 2 tbsps milk or 4 tbsps
    soya flour mixed with 3 tbsps water
½ tsp mixed herbs
½ tsp dried mustard
Salt and pepper

Topping
A little olive oil
1 tbsp tomato purée
50g/2oz margarine
1 large onion, finely chopped
100g/4oz mushrooms, sliced
1 green or red pepper, finely sliced
4 tomatoes, sliced
2 sticks celery, finely sliced
100g/4oz Cheddar cheese, grated

1. Make the scone mix by rubbing the margarine into the flour until it resembles fine breadcrumbs.

2. Beat the eggs together with the milk.

3. Add to the flour mixture together with the herbs, mustard and seasoning. Knead together to form a ball of dough.

4. Press the mixture evenly over a 25.4cm/ 10" pizza plate.

5. Brush the top with a little olive oil and spread the tomato purée evenly over the top with a knife.

6. Melt the margarine in a frying pan and cook the onions, mushrooms, pepper and celery for 4-5 minutes until softened a little.

7. Pile the mixture on top of the pizza base.

8. Lay the tomatoes evenly over the top and sprinkle on the grated cheese.

9. Bake for 20-25 minutes at 200°C/400°F/ Gas Mark 6 until the cheese is melted and golden brown.

TIME: Preparation takes 20 minutes, cooking takes about 30 minutes.

SERVING IDEA: Garnish with watercress and serve with sweetcorn or a crisp green salad.

FREEZING: Freeze after cooking for up to 2 months. Allow to thaw before reheating in the oven.

175

EXPRESS VEGETABLE PIE

*Any cooked, left-over vegetables may be
used for this quick and easy pie.*

SERVES 4

1 large onion, peeled and finely chopped
25g/1oz margarine
2 sticks of celery, diced
75g/3oz cashew nuts, chopped and dry
    roasted
675g/1½ lbs mixed frozen vegetables
    (peas, corn, swede, carrot, turnip, diced
    peppers, parsnip etc.)
1 dstsp tomato purée
140ml/¼ pint water or stock
½ -1 tsp yeast extract
Salt and black pepper
3-4 large potatoes
Knob of butter
Little milk

1. Sauté the onion in the margarine
together with the celery and a little water
until just tender.

2. Add the remaining ingredients apart
from the potatoes, butter and milk.

3. Simmer for 3-5 minutes, adding a little
more water if the mixture seems too dry.
Keep hot.

4. Cook the potatoes until soft, mash with
a knob of butter and a little milk, adding
salt and pepper to taste.

5. Turn the vegetable mixture into a
casserole dish and cover completely with
the mashed potato.

6. Fork over the top roughly, dot with
butter and grill for 3-5 minutes until
golden brown.

7. Serve immediately.

TIME: Preparation takes 20 minutes, cooking takes 15 minutes.

SERVING IDEA: Serve with salad, mushrooms and pumpkin seeds.

SAVOURY RICE CAKE

An excellent way to use up left-over rice.

SERVES 2-4

1 medium onion, finely chopped
1 clove garlic, crushed
2 tbsps olive oil
1 tbsp fresh thyme, chopped
1 red pepper, thinly sliced
1 green pepper, thinly sliced
4 eggs, beaten
Salt and pepper
6 tbsps cooked brown rice
3 tbsps natural yogurt
75g/3oz Cheddar cheese, grated

1. Fry the onion and garlic in the olive oil until soft.

2. Add the thyme and pepper and fry gently for 4-5 minutes.

3. Beat the eggs with the salt and pepper.

4. Add the cooked rice to the thyme and pepper followed by the eggs.

5. Cook over a moderate heat, stirring from time to time until the eggs are cooked underneath.

6. Spoon the yogurt on top of the part-set egg and sprinkle the cheese over the top.

7. Put under a moderate grill and cook until puffed and golden.

8. Serve immediately.

TIME: Preparation takes about 15 minutes, cooking takes 15 minutes.

SERVING IDEA: Garnish with fresh thyme and serve with a green salad.

QUICK VEGETABLE CHILLI

Serve this tasty chilli with wholemeal baps and salad.

SERVES 4

2 large onions, sliced
1 tbsp olive oil
¾ cloves garlic, crushed
1 tsp chilli powder
400g/1 x 14oz tin tomatoes, chopped
400g/1 x 14oz tin of red kidney beans
1 small red pepper, roughly chopped
1 medium courgette, sliced into chunks
Cauliflower florets
2 carrots, roughly chopped
½ tbsp tomato purée
1 tsp dried, sweet basil
1 tsp oregano
¼ -½ pint stock

1. Sauté the onions in the oil until soft.

2. Add the garlic and cook for 1 minute.

3. Add the chilli powder and cook for a further minute.

4. Add the rest of the ingredients and simmer for 25-30 minutes.

5. Serve on a bed of brown rice.

TIME: Preparation takes about 15 minutes, cooking takes 30 minutes.

VARIATION: Florets of broccoli could be used in place of the cauliflower.

SPEEDY PIZZA

The perfect meal in a hurry.

SERVES 4-6

Pastry
225g/8oz wholemeal self-raising flour
75g/3oz vegetable suet
Scant ½ tsp salt
Cold water to mix, approx. 225ml/8fl.oz

Filling
Olive oil
1 tbsp tomato purée
1 medium onion, very finely chopped
1 x 400g/14oz tin artichokes, halved
6 medium tomatoes, skinned and sliced
1 tsp dried oregano
100g/4oz Cheddar cheese, finely sliced
12 black olives, stoned and halved
   (optional)

1. Mix the flour, salt and suet together in a large bowl and add enough cold water to make a pliable dough.

2. Roll out into a 25cm/10" round and place on a greased baking sheet.

3. Brush with olive oil and cover with the tomato purée.

4. Arrange the onion, artichokes and tomatoes on the top.

5. Sprinkle with oregano.

6. Arrange the cheese over the mixture and place the olives on the top.

7. Bake at 190°C/375°F/Gas Mark 5 for about 35 minutes.

TIME: Preparation takes 10 minutes, cooking takes 35 minutes.

SERVING IDEA: Serve with jacket potatoes and a crisp salad.

VARIATION: Courgettes or mushrooms may be used in place of the artichokes.
Basil or mixed herbs can take the place of the oregano.

WATCHPOINT: Make sure that you chop the onions very finely or they will not cook.
Alternatively, if you have time, you can pre-cook the onions a little
before putting on top of the pizza.

COURGETTES MEDITERRANEAN STYLE

Any other type of cooked bean may be used for this dish.

SERVES 4

3 tbsps olive oil
1 large onion, finely chopped
3 cloves garlic, crushed
1 red pepper, chopped
225g/8oz cooked haricot beans
1 x 400g/14oz tin tomatoes
450g/1lb courgettes, finely sliced
1 level tsp oregano
Seasoning

1. Heat the oil in a pan.

2. Add the onion, garlic and pepper and cook for 4-5 minutes.

3. Add the cooked beans, tinned tomatoes and courgettes. Stir well.

4. Add the oregano and seasoning, and stir again.

5. Cover and cook slowly for 30 minutes.

TIME: Preparation takes 10-15 minutes, cooking takes 40 minutes.

SERVING IDEA: Serve on a bed of white rice.

COOK'S TIP: This dish will reheat well.

OVEN BAKED SPAGHETTI

A convenient way to cook this favourite mid-week meal.

SERVES 4

225g/8oz wholewheat spaghetti, cooked
2 x 400g/14oz tins tomatoes, roughly
  chopped
1 large onion, grated
1 tsp oregano
Seasoning
100g/4oz Cheddar cheese
2 tbsps Parmesan cheese, grated

1. Grease four individual ovenproof dishes and place a quarter of the spaghetti in each one.

2. Pour the tomatoes over the top.

3. Add the onion, sprinkle with oregano and season well.

4. Slice the cheese finely and arrange over the top of the spaghetti mixture.

5. Sprinkle with Parmesan and bake at 180°C/350°F/Gas Mark 4 for 30 minutes.

TIME: Preparation takes 10 minutes, cooking takes 20-25 minutes.

SERVING IDEA: Serve with garlic bread.

WATCHPOINT: When cooking spaghetti remember to add a few drops of oil to the boiling water to stop it sticking together.

COOK'S TIP: Oven Baked Spaghetti may be cooked in one large casserole if required but add 10 minutes to the cooking time.

TOMATO AND PEPPER QUICHE

Quiche is tastiest served with jacket potatoes and a crisp salad.

SERVES 4

Pastry case
100g/4oz wholewheat flour
Pinch of salt
50g/2oz vegetable fat
A little cold water to mix

Filling
25g/1oz butter or margarine
1 onion, finely chopped
½ green pepper, finely sliced
½ red pepper, finely sliced
2 tomatoes, finely sliced
3 eggs
280ml/½ pint single cream
Seasoning
2 tbsps Parmesan cheese

1. Mix the flour and salt together.

2. Cut the fat into small pieces and rub into the flour until the mixture resembles fine breadcrumbs.

3. Add the water and mix until a ball of dough is formed.

4. Roll out to line a 20cm/8" flan tin or quiche dish.

5. Prick the bottom lightly with a fork and cook at 180°C/350°F/Gas Mark 4 for 15 minutes.

6. Remove from the oven.

7. Meanwhile, melt the butter or margarine in a frying pan and sauté the onion and pepper until just softened.

8. Arrange the onion and pepper on the bottom of the pastry case followed by the sliced tomatoes.

9. Beat the eggs, and add the cream and seasoning.

10. Pour over the vegetables and sprinkle the cheese on top.

11. Return to the oven for 35-40 minutes until risen and golden brown on top.

TIME: Preparation takes 25 minutes, cooking takes 55 minutes.

VARIATION: For an everyday quiche, replace the cream with milk.

LENTIL MOUSSAKA

Try a taste of the Greek Islands with this classic dish.

SERVES 4-6

150g/5oz green lentils
1 large aubergine, sliced
4-5 tbsps oil
1 large onion, chopped
1 clove garlic, crushed
1 large carrot, diced
4 sticks celery, finely chopped
1-2 tsps mixed herbs
1 x 400g/14oz tin tomatoes
1 dstsp shoyu sauce (Japanese soy sauce)
Black pepper
2 medium potatoes, cooked and sliced
2 large tomatoes, sliced

Sauce
50g/2oz margarine
50g/2oz brown rice flour
425ml/¾ pint milk
1 large egg, separated
50g/2oz grated Cheddar cheese
1 tsp nutmeg

1. Cook the lentils in plenty of water until soft. Drain and reserve the liquid.

2. Fry the aubergine in the oil, drain well and set aside.

3. Sauté the onion, garlic, carrot, celery and a little of the lentil stock.

4. Simmer with the lid on until just tender.

5. Add the lentils, mixed herbs and tinned tomatoes. Simmer gently for 3-4 minutes.

6. Season with the shoyu and pepper.

7. Place a layer of the lentil mixture in a large casserole dish and cover with half of the aubergine slices.

8. Cover the aubergine slices with half of the potato slices and all the tomato.

9. Repeat with the remaining lentils, aubergines and potatoes.

10. To make the sauce, melt the margarine in a saucepan, remove from the heat and stir in the flour to make a roux.

11. Add the milk gradually, blending well, so that the sauce is smooth and lump free.

12. Return to the heat and stir continually until the sauce thickens.

13. Remove the pan from the heat and cool slightly. Add the egg yolk, stir in the cheese and add the nutmeg.

14. Beat the egg white until it is stiff, then carefully fold into the sauce.

15. Pour the sauce over the moussaka, covering the dish completely.

16. Bake at 180°C/350°F/Gas Mark 4 for about 40 minutes until the top is golden brown and puffy.

TIME: Preparation takes 45 minutes, cooking takes 1 hour 10 minutes.

FREEZING: Assemble the mixture without the sauce and freeze. Defrost, add the sauce and cook from Step 14.

SERVING IDEA: Serve with a crunchy green salad or battered mushrooms.

SPAGHETTI BOLOGNAISE

Any cooked beans can be used in this recipe.

SERVES 2-4

350/12oz wholewheat spaghetti
4 tbsps olive oil
225g/8oz onions, chopped
1 clove garlic, crushed
1 x 400g/14oz tin tomatoes, chopped and
    juice retained
100g/4oz carrots, diced
2 sticks celery, sliced
100g/4oz mushrooms, sliced
1 small red pepper, diced
½ tsp basil
½ tsp oregano
¼ tsp nutmeg
2 tbsps tomato purée
280ml/½ pint stock or water
175g/6oz cooked aduki beans
2 tsps soya flour
Salt and pepper
Parmesan cheese

1. Cook the spaghetti as per the instructions on the packet.

2. Heat the olive oil in a large pan and cook the onions and garlic until browned.

3. Add the tinned tomatoes with their juice, the carrots, celery, mushrooms, pepper, basil, oregano, nutmeg, tomato purée, and stock.

4. Stir well and simmer for about 20 minutes or until the vegetables are cooked.

5. Add the cooked beans and cook for a further 5 minutes.

6. Mix the soya flour with a little water and add to the sauce and allow to cook for 2 minutes.

7. Season to taste.

8. Drain the spaghetti and serve topped with the bolognaise sauce and a sprinkling of Parmesan cheese.

TIME: Preparation takes about 30 minutes, cooking takes 35 minutes.

COOK'S TIP: Add a tablespoon of oil to the water in which the spaghetti is cooked to prevent it from sticking together.

VEGETARIAN PAELLA

Perfect served with crusty bread and a green salad.

SERVES 4-6

4 tbsps olive oil
1 large onion, chopped
2 cloves garlic, crushed
½ tsp paprika
350g/12oz long grain brown rice
1150ml/1½ pints stock
175ml/6fl.oz dry white wine
1 x 400g/14oz tin tomatoes, plus juice,
    chopped
1 tbsp tomato purée
½ tsp tarragon
1 tsp basil
1 tsp oregano
1 red pepper, roughly chopped
1 green pepper, roughly chopped
3 sticks celery, finely chopped
225g/8oz mushrooms, washed and sliced
50g/2oz mange tout, topped and tailed
    and cut into halves
100g/4oz frozen peas
50g/2oz cashew nut pieces
Salt and pepper

1. Heat the oil and fry the onion and garlic until soft.

2. Add the paprika and rice and continue to cook for 4-5 minutes until the rice is transparent. Stir occasionally.

3. Add the stock, wine, tomatoes, tomato purée and herbs and simmer for 10-15 minutes.

4. Add the pepper, celery, mushrooms and mange tout and continue to cook for another 30 minutes until the rice is cooked.

5. Add the peas, cashew nuts and seasoning to taste.

6. Heat through and place on a large heated serving dish.

7. Sprinkle the parsley over the top and garnish with lemon wedges and olives.

TIME: Preparation takes 20 minutes, cooking takes 45 minutes.

COOK'S TIP: To prepare in advance, undercook slightly, add a little more stock or water and reheat. Do not add the peas until just before serving otherwise they will lose their colour.

MOORS AND CHRISTIANS

*This dish, originally from Cuba, is so called
because of the use of black beans and white rice.*

SERVES 4

225g/8oz black beans, soaked overnight
  and cooked until soft
2 tbsps vegetable oil
1 medium onion, chopped
4 cloves garlic, crushed
1 medium green pepper, finely chopped
2 large tomatoes, skinned and finely
  chopped
275g/10oz long grain rice
Salt and pepper
Little bean cooking water if required

1. Drain the cooked beans and mash 3
tbsps to a paste with a fork, adding a little
bean cooking water if necesssary.

2. Heat the oil and fry the onion, garlic
and pepper until soft.

3. Add the tomatoes and cook for a
further 2 minutes.

4. Add the bean paste and stir.

5. Add the cooked beans and rice, and
enough water to cover.

6. Bring to the boil, cover and simmer for
20-25 minutes until the rice is *al dente*.

7. Serve hot.

TIME: Preparation takes 15 minutes. Cooking time, 1-1½ hours for the beans, 25-30
minutes for the finished dish.

SERVING IDEA: Serve with a crisp green salad and crusty bread.

VARIATION: A small tin of tomatoes may be used in place of fresh ones.

PULSES, GRAINS & PASTA

Pulses used to be considered food for the underprivileged, but in recent years their true nutritional value has been recognised and we are now lucky to find a wide selection available – as many as 25 different types – providing a variety of cheap and nutritious dishes.

Dried beans contain protein, vitamins, minerals and fibre and are particularly high in vitamins B1 and B2. They also contain significant amounts of calcium, phosphorous, and iron. Dried pulses should always be washed thoroughly before use. Leave them to stand in water for the time recommended on the packet. Once the pulses have been soaked, transfer to a saucepan and cover with fresh water. Bring to the boil and boil rapidly for the first 10 minutes, turn down the heat and continue boiling slowly until the beans are cooked. To test, remove a bean from the pot, hold between thumb and forefinger and squeeze gently. If the bean yields to the pressure it should be soft enough to eat.

Grains are another important food group. These botanic grasses are the staple food of most of the world, and are the cheapest, most important source of energy. A wide variety of grains are available, but the majority of people still tend to use only a small proportion of them, such as pearl barley, oats and rice. There are many other delicious grains to choose from. Millet, for instance, can be made into a breakfast dish, bulgar salad makes a nice change from rice salad, and buckwheat is excellent in casseroles and roasts.

Home-made pasta is a delight and far superior to its shop-bought relatives. This chapter includes two recipes for fresh pasta which you can incorporate into your repertoire and once you've made your own pasta you'll never want to buy it again.

BLACK AND WHITE BAKE WITH BOULANGERE TOPPING

Serve this hearty dish with lightly steamed vegetables.

SERVES 4

100g/4oz black kidney beans, soaked
   overnight and cooked until tender
1 medium cauliflower, divided into florets
700ml/1¼ pints water
1 bay leaf
280ml/½ pint milk
2 tbsps sunflower oil
1 medium onion, very finely chopped
40g/1½ oz fine wholemeal flour
1 tbsp wholegrain mustard
1 tbsp parsley, chopped
Salt and pepper
350-450g/¾ -1lb potatoes, cooked and cut
   into 5mm/¼ " slices
25g/1oz butter or margarine

---

1. Wash and drain the cauliflower florets.

2. Bring the water to the boil in a large pan, add the bay leaf and a little salt.

3. Plunge the cauliflower into the water, return to the boil, cover and poach the florets for 8-10 minutes until just cooked.

4. Drain, discard the bay leaf and reserve the cooking water.

5. Top up the milk with the cooking water to give 570ml/1 pint.

6. Heat the oil in a small pan and gently sauté the onion until soft.

7. Stir in the flour and cook over a gentle heat for 1-2 minutes.

8. Gradually add the milk and water, stirring all the time to avoid lumps.

9. Add the mustard and cook gently for a further 3 minutes.

10. Drain the cooked beans and return them to a large pan, add the florets and mix well.

11. Pour the mustard sauce over the beans and cauliflower and stir in the chopped parsley and seasoning.

12. Place the mixture in a greased 1½ ltr/3 pint casserole dish.

13. Top with the sliced potatoes, overlapping them slightly, and dot with the butter or margarine.

14. Bake at 180°C/350°/Gas Mark 4 for 20-25 minutes until the top is nicely browned.

TIME: Preparation takes 25 minutes. Cooking time, including the beans, 1 hour 10 minutes.

FREEZING: Freeze the base for 4-6 weeks and add the topping when required.

COOK'S TIP: Choosing the right sort of topping for bakes is most important, it should enhance what is underneath rather than fighting against it.

VEGETARIAN SHEPHERD'S PIE

*The Shepherds Pie will serve 2 people without
any accompaniments and 4 people if served with vegetables.*

SERVES 2-4

100g/4oz brown lentils
50g/2oz pot barley
450ml/¾ pint stock or water
1 tsp yeast extract
1 large carrot, diced
½ onion, chopped finely
1 clove garlic, crushed
50g/2oz walnuts, roughly chopped
1 tsp vegetarian gravy powder or
    thickener
Salt and pepper
450g/1lb potatoes, cooked and mashed

1. Simmer the lentils and barley in 280ml/
½ pint of the stock and yeast extract for
30 minutes.

2. Meanwhile, cook the carrot, onion,
garlic and walnuts in the remaining stock
for 15 minutes or until tender.

3. Mix the gravy powder or thickener with
a little water and add to the carrot
mixture, stir over a low heat until
thickened.

4. Combine the lentils and barley with the
carrot mixture, season and place in an
ovenproof dish.

5. Cover with the mashed potato and cook
at 180°C/350°F/Gas Mark 4 for about 30
minutes until browned on top.

TIME: Preparation takes 15 minutes, cooking takes 1 hour.

SERVING IDEA: Garnish with grilled tomatoes and serve with vegetables in season,
broccoli, sprouts, spring cabbage etc.

BUCKWHEAT SAVOURY

*Garnish this tasty recipe with fronds of fennel
and serve with a fennel and orange salad.*

SERVES 4

1 tbsp sultanas
1 medium onion, finely chopped
1-2 cloves garlic, crushed
2 sticks celery, finely chopped
Oil
1-2 tsps garam masala
¼ tsp ground cumin
100g/4oz buckwheat
2 medium carrots, diced
1 small red pepper, diced
75g/3oz cashew nuts, roughly chopped
1 dstsp tomato purée
1 tsp yeast extract or bouillon powder
   dissolved in 1 cup boiling water
Salt and pepper
2 courgettes, cut into bite-sized pieces

1. Soak the sultanas in a little water for about 1 hour.

2. Place the onion, garlic and celery in a saucepan with a little oil and sauté together for about 4 minutes.

3. Add the garam masala and cumin and cook for a further minute.

4. Add the remaining ingredients, except the sultanas and courgettes.

5. Simmer for about 20 minutes or until the buckwheat is soft and chewy but do not allow the mixture to become too dry.

6. Add the sultanas and courgettes and cook for a further 5 minutes. The courgettes should not be allowed to become too soft.

7. Transfer to a heated serving dish and serve at once.

TIME: Preparation takes 15 minutes, soaking takes 1 hour and cooking takes 30 minutes.

VARIATION: Any leftover mixture can be used as a stuffing for peppers. Bake the peppers for about 20 minutes, fill and place in a covered dish. Bake for a further 10 minutes until piping hot.

BULGAR RISOTTO

*This makes a quick lunch dish and is
particularly handy if unexpected guests call.*

SERVES 3-4

100g/4oz bulgar wheat
1 medium onion, peeled and finely
    chopped
2 sticks celery, finely chopped
1-2 cloves garlic, crushed
12g/½ oz butter
1 small red pepper, diced
1 small green pepper, diced
½ tsp dried mixed herbs
50g/2oz peanuts, chopped
1 tsp vegetable extract dissolved in ¼ cup
    boiling water
2 tsps shoyu sauce (Japanese soy sauce)
75g/3oz sweetcorn
75g/3oz peas
Salt and pepper
Juice of half a lemon

1. Put the bulgar wheat into a bowl and
cover with boiling water.

2. Leave for about 10 minutes after which
time the water will have been absorbed
and the wheat swollen.

3. Meanwhile, place the onion, celery and
garlic into a saucepan and sauté for a few
minutes in the butter.

4. Add the peppers, herbs, nuts and
vegetable extract.

5. Simmer over a low heat for about 8
minutes.

6. Add the bulgar wheat, shoyu,
sweetcorn, peas and seasoning and mix
together well.

7. Continue cooking for a further 5
minutes.

8. Mix in the lemon juice and transfer to a
heated serving dish.

9. Serve immediately.

TIME: Preparation takes 15 minutes, cooking takes 20 minutes.

SERVING IDEA: Serve with a crisp green salad.

WATCHPOINT: If the risotto is too dry, add a little more water or stock.

MILLET RISSOLES WITH YOGURT SAUCE

*Rissoles are always popular and yogurt
sauce makes these even more tempting!*

MAKES ABOUT 15

1 medium onion, peeled and finely
    chopped
1 clove garlic, crushed
1 tsp dried mixed herbs or 2 tbsps freshly
    chopped parsley
Oil
150g/5oz millet flakes
300-450ml/½ -¾ pint water
1 tbsp tomato purée
1 tsp vegetable extract
75g/3oz Cheddar cheese, grated
¼ tsp paprika
Salt and pepper
Wholemeal breadcrumbs

Sauce
10fl.oz/½ pint Greek yogurt
2 tbsps freshly chopped parsley
Salt and pepper
Pinch of paprika
A little lemon juice (optional)

1. Sauté the onion, garlic and mixed herbs in a little oil until soft.

2. Place the millet flakes in a separate pan with the water, bring to the boil and simmer gently, stirring constantly until a thick texture results.

3. Cool a little.

4. Add the remaining rissole ingredients, except the breadcrumbs, and mix together well.

5. Shape into rissoles and coat with the crumbs.

6. Fry in very shallow oil on both sides until crisp and golden.

7. To make the sauce, mix all the ingredients together well.

TIME: Preparation takes 15 minutes, cooking takes 15 minutes.

SERVING IDEA: Serve with the sauce handed round separately.

VARIATION: Vary the flavour of the rissoles by using freshly chopped
mint instead of the mixed herbs or parsley.
Fresh basil also makes a delicious alternative.

MILLET MEDLEY

A tasty and wholesome recipe for the whole family.

SERVES 4

1 medium onion, chopped
2 tbsps oil
225g/8oz millet
570ml/1 pint stock or water
Salt and pepper
75g/3oz cooked peas
75g/3oz sweetcorn
4 sticks celery, chopped
50g/2oz sunflower seeds
2 tbsps shoyu sauce (Japanese soy sauce)

1. Sauté the onion in the oil for 2-3 minutes.

2. Add the dry millet and cook for a few minutes, stirring all the time.

3. Add the stock and seasoning, bring to the boil and simmer over a low heat for 30 minutes.

4. Allow to cool.

5. Add the peas, sweetcorn and celery and mix well.

6. Place the sunflower seeds and shoyu into a frying pan and cook over a medium heat, stirring continuously until the seeds are dry. Cool.

7. Just before serving, sprinkle with the toasted sunflower seeds.

TIME: Preparation takes 10 minutes, cooking takes 40 minutes.

SERVING IDEA: Serve garnished with tomatoes.

VARIATION: Replace the sunflower seeds with pumpkin seeds.

PEANUT RISOTTO

Use this mixture to stuff cabbage, spinach or vine leaves.

SERVES 4

---

1 large onion, chopped
1 clove garlic, crushed
1 tbsp vegetable oil
150g/6oz short grain brown rice
100g/4oz peanuts, roughly chopped
100g/4oz mushrooms, sliced
570ml/1 pint boiling water
100g/4oz fine beans
25g/1oz raisins
2 tsps dried oregano
2 tsps lemon juice
Salt and pepper

1. Fry the onion and garlic in the oil for 3-4 minutes.

2. Add the rice and peanuts to toast for 1-2 minutes.

3. Add the mushrooms and cook for a further 3-4 minutes, then add the boiling water, stir once and simmer for 30 minutes.

4. Add the beans, raisins, herbs, lemon juice and seasoning and cook for a further 5-10 minutes.

TIME: Preparation takes 10 minutes, cooking takes 50 minutes.

SERVING IDEA: Serve garnished with lemon wedges and parsley.

VARIATION: Use this mixture to stuff cabbage, spinach or vine leaves.

SAVOURY GRAIN CASSEROLE

*Serve as a complete meal for 2 people or serve
accompanied with lightly steamed vegetables for 4 people.*

SERVES 2-4

75g/3oz brown rice
75g/3oz split peas
2 sticks celery, very finely chopped
1 medium onion, very finely chopped
100g/4oz mushrooms, chopped
1 x 400g/14oz tin tomatoes, drained and
　chopped or 225g/8oz tomatoes, peeled
　and chopped
½ tsp dill seeds
½ tsp thyme
2 tbsps shoyu sauce (Japanese soy sauce)
1 egg, beaten
100g/4oz Cheddar cheese, grated

1. Cover the rice with water and cook for
10-15 minutes; drain.

2. Cover the split peas with water and
cook for 20 minutes until just tender but
not mushy; drain.

3. Meanwhile, combine the celery, onion,
mushrooms, tomatoes, dill, thyme, shoyu
and the egg in a large bowl.

4. Stir in the rice and peas.

5. Place the mixture in a greased
ovenproof casserole dish and cook for 45
minutes at 180°C/350°F/Gas Mark 4.

6. Remove from the oven and sprinkle
with the grated cheese.

7. Return to the oven for 10 minutes until
the cheese has melted.

8. Serve at once.

TIME: Preparation takes 10 minutes, cooking takes 1 hour 45 minutes.

SERVING IDEA: Garnish with a few whole cooked button mushrooms or grilled tomatoes.

WHOLEWHEAT PASTA

Home-made pasta is always superior to the shop-bought varieties.

MAKES 450G/1lb

275g/10oz plain wholewheat flour
Large pinch of salt
3 eggs
15ml/1 tbsp olive oil

1. Put the flour and salt into a large mixing bowl or heap on a pastry board, make a well in the centre and break in the eggs and add the olive oil.

2. Mix together with a fork until the dough can be gathered into a rough ball. If the dough is too dry and will not come together, add a few drops of water.

3. Knead the dough well for 5-10 minutes, incorporating all the flour left on the board, until it is smooth, shiny and no longer sticky.

4. Cover the dough with cling film and leave to rest in a cool place for half an hour.

5. Divide the dough into two, wrapping one half in cling film to stop it drying out.

6. Lightly flour the working surface and rolling pin and roll out the dough as thinly as possible, turning and dusting with flour underneath as for pastry. The pasta should be thin enough to be able to see the shadow of a hand against it when held up to the light.

TIME: Preparation takes 20 minutes.

FREEZING: Freeze for up to three months. De-frost and use as for fresh pasta.

216

SPINACH PASTA

This tasty and colourful pasta can be used
in numerous Italian dishes.

MAKES 450G/1lb

275g/10oz plain wholewheat flour
Large pinch of salt
2 eggs
100g/4oz cooked spinach, finely chopped
15ml/1 tbsp olive oil

1. Put the flour and salt into a large mixing bowl or heap on a pastry board, make a well in the centre.

2. Mix the eggs with the spinach and pour this into the centre of the flour along with the olive oil.

3. Mix together with a fork until the dough can be gathered into a rough ball.

4. Add a little water or extra oil if the dough is a little dry.

5. Roll out in the same way as whole wheat pasta and use as you would pre-packed pasta.

TIME: Preparation takes 20 minutes.

FREEZING: Freeze for up to three months. De-frost and use as for fresh pasta.

VARIATIONS: Tomato Pasta – Replace one of the eggs with 3 tbsps of tomato purée for a delicate 'pink' pasta.
Saffron Pasta – Use two eggs plus two egg yolks and 1 tsp saffron powder. This gives a golden colour which will show better if the wholewheat flour is replaced with unbleached plain flour in the same quantity.

SPICY BLACK-EYED BEANS

A spicy dish from the West Indies.

SERVES 4

225g/8oz black-eyed beans, soaked and cooked
4 tbsps vegetable oil
1 large onion, finely chopped
2 cloves garlic, crushed
1 tsp ground cinnamon
½ tsp ground cumin
Salt and pepper
140ml/5fl.oz/¼ pint bean stock or water
2 tbsps tomato purée
1 tbsp shoyu sauce (Japanese soy sauce)
2 large tomatoes, skinned and chopped
1 tbsp chopped parsley

1. Drain the beans well and retain the cooking liquid.

2. Heat the oil and fry the onion and garlic for 4-5 minutes until soft.

3. Stir in the cinnamon, cumin and seasoning and cook for a further 2 minutes.

4. Add the beans, bean stock, tomato purée, shoyu sauce and tomatoes.

5. Stir and bring to the boil.

6. Simmer for 15-20 minutes until thick.

7. Check the seasoning.

8. Serve poured over cooked pasta and sprinkled with chopped parsley.

TIME: Preparation takes 20 minutes. Cooking time, including the beans, 1 hour 35 minutes.

SERVING IDEA: Serve over cooked rice and garnish with lemon wedges.

VARIATION: Haricot beans can be used in place of black-eyed beans.

221

BUTTER BEAN AND SPINACH ROLL WITH LEMON CRUST

The lemon crust gives just the right edge of flavour to make the whole dish a little bit special.

SERVES 4

225g/8oz butter beans, soaked overnight
  and cooked until tender
225g/8oz fresh spinach
½ tsp freshly grated nutmeg
Salt and freshly ground black pepper
50g/2oz Cheddar cheese, grated
1 egg, beaten
1 tsp sunflower oil
50g/2oz fresh breadcrumbs
1 tbsp sesame seeds
Grated rind of 1 lemon
2 tsps lemon juice

---

1. Preheat the oven to 200°C/400°F/Gas Mark 6.

2. Drain the cooked beans, transfer to a large bowl and mash well.

3. Wash and trim the spinach. Using a pan with a close fitting lid, cook the spinach, with no added water, for 5 minutes.

4. When cooked and cool enough to handle, chop the spinach finely and add the nutmeg and seasoning.

5. Stir the grated cheese and beaten egg into the mashed butterbeans.

6. Place a sheet of cling film on the working surface and spread the bean mixture over it in a rectangle measuring roughly 17.8cm x 27.9cm/7" x 11".

7. Cover the bean layer with the chopped spinach.

8. With the short end towards you, lift the edge of the cling film and gently roll the mixture into a cylinder, using the film to support the roll.

9. In a bowl, rub the oil into the breadcrumbs and stir in the sesame seeds and lemon rind.

10. Spread the breadcrumb mixture over the working surface and roll the butter bean roll over it until it is well covered.

11. Transfer the roll to a greased baking sheet, sprinkle with the lemon juice and bake for 15-20 minutes until the crust is crisp and golden.

TIME: Preparation takes 15 minutes. Cooking time, including the beans, 1 hour 30 minutes.

SERVING IDEA: Serve with a colourful mixed pepper salad.

BUTTER BEANS AND MUSHROOMS AU GRATIN

*You can vary the flavour of this dish by
substituting other kinds of beans.*

SERVES 4

175g/6oz butter beans, soaked overnight
 and cooked until soft
75g/3oz butter
1 tbsp lemon juice
Salt and pepper
225g/8oz mushrooms, separate the caps
 from the stalks
25g/1oz wholemeal breadcrumbs
25g/1oz grated cheese
Sauce
50g/2oz margarine
50g/2oz flour
280ml/½ pint milk

1. Mix the beans with 50g/2oz of the
butter, lemon juice and salt and pepper.

2. Place the mixture in the bottom of a pie
dish.

3. Melt the remaining butter in a pan and
fry the mushroom caps for about 5
minutes.

4. Make the sauce by melting the
margarine and stirring in the flour, cook
for about 2 minutes and then gradually
add the milk, stirring all the time until the
sauce thickens.

5. Chop the mushroom stalks and add to
the sauce, pour this over the beans.

6. Place the cooked mushroom caps,
underside upwards, on the top and
sprinkle with the breadcrumbs and
cheese.

7. Bake in a moderate oven, 190°C/375°F/
Gas Mark 5, for about 15 minutes until the
top is brown.

TIME: Preparation takes 15 minutes, cooking takes 35 minutes.

SERVING IDEA: Serve with lightly steamed green vegetables.

CHICKPEA STEW

*You can use tinned chickpeas for this recipe
but the dried ones have a much nicer flavour.*

SERVES 4

1 large onion, finely chopped
1 large carrot, diced
1 tbsp vegetable oil
2 large potatoes, peeled and diced
400g/1 x 14oz tin of tomatoes
1 tsp dried basil
Freshly ground black pepper
225g/8oz cooked chickpeas

1. Place the onion, carrot and oil in a pan and fry gently for about 5 minutes.

2. Add the potatoes, tomatoes and their juice, herbs and pepper.

3. Cover and simmer gently for about 30 minutes or until the potatoes are soft. Stir occasionally to make sure that the potatoes do not stick to the bottom of the pan.

4. Add the cooked chickpeas and warm through gently.

TIME: Preparation takes about 20 minutes, cooking takes 35-40 minutes.

SERVING IDEA: Serve with cooked green vegetables such as broccoli, peas or spring cabbage.

CHANA MASALA

*An excellent dish to serve hot as a main course or cold
as an accompaniment to a nut loaf.*

SERVES 4

---

1 large onion, chopped
4 cloves garlic, crushed
2.5cm/¾ " fresh ginger, peeled and finely
    chopped
3 tbsps ghee
1 tbsp ground coriander
2 tsps cumin seed
¼ tsp cayenne pepper
1 tsp turmeric
2 tsps roasted cumin seed, ground
1 tbsp amchur (dried mango powder) or 1
    tbsp lemon juice
2 tsps paprika
400g/1 x 14oz tin Italian tomatoes
675g/1½ lbs cooked chickpeas
    (12oz uncooked)
1 tsp garam masala
½ tsp salt
1 fresh green chilli, finely chopped

1. Sauté the onion, garlic and ginger in the ghee until soft.

2. Add all the spices and fry over a low heat for 1-2 minutes stirring all the time.

3. Add the tomatoes, roughly chopped, together with their juice.

4. Add the cooked chickpeas.

5. Cook for 30 minutes over a medium heat.

6. Add the garam masala, salt and chilli, stir well and serve.

TIME: Preparation takes about 15 minutes, cooking takes 30 minutes.

SERVING IDEA: Serve hot with coconut rice and mango chutney. This dish improves with time and is always more flavourful the following day.

WATCHPOINT: Fry the spices over a low heat to ensure they do not burn.

VARIATION: Small pieces of diced vegetables such as potatoes, fresh tomatoes or cauliflower may be added.

CHICKPEA BURGERS

*These burgers are nice cold and are
useful for a packed lunch or picnic.*

SERVES 4

450g/1lb cooked chickpeas or 2 x 14oz
  cans chickpeas
1 onion, finely chopped
2 cloves garlic, crushed
2 medium potatoes, cooked and mashed
2 tbsps shoyu sauce (Japanese soy sauce)
1 dstsp lemon juice
Black pepper
Wholewheat flour
Oil for frying

1. Put the chickpeas into a large bowl and
mash well.

2. Add the onion, garlic, potato, shoyu,
lemon juice and pepper. Mix together
well.

3. With floured hands, shape heaped
tablespoonfuls of the mixture into small
burgers.

4. Coat each burger with flour and
refrigerate for 1 hour.

5. Heat a little oil and gently fry the
burgers on each side until golden brown.

TIME: Preparation takes 15 minutes, cooking takes about 15 minutes.

SERVING IDEA: Serve with a hot, spicy tomato sauce.

FREEZING: Cook and freeze for up to 2 months.

CHESTNUT HOT-POT

This enticing hot-pot is perfect served with a lightly cooked green vegetable.

SERVES 4-6

675g/1½ lbs potatoes
3 medium onions
225g/8oz brown lentils
225g/8oz chestnuts
Salt and pepper
1 dstsp yeast extract
430ml/¾ pint warm water
50g/2oz margarine

1. Peel and slice the potatoes and onions thinly.

2. Put layers of potatoes, onions, lentils and chestnuts into a greased pie dish ending with a layer of potatoes. Season well between each layer.

3. Dissolve the yeast extract in the warm water and pour over.

4. Dot with margarine and cover.

5. Bake at 190°C/375°F/Gas Mark 4 for an hour or until the potatoes are tender.

6. Turn up the oven to 200°C/400°F/Gas Mark 6, remove the lid from the casserole and return to the oven for 10-15 minutes until the potatoes are crispy and golden brown.

TIME: Preparation takes 20 minutes, cooking takes 1 hour 15 minutes.

VARIATION: Dried chestnuts may be used but need to be soaked overnight in stock or water.

GREEN LENTILS WITH FRESH GINGER AND SPICES

There's certainly no lack of taste in this spicy lentil mix.

SERVES 4

175g/6oz green or Continental lentils
Water or stock to cover
25g/1oz margarine or 1 tbsp soya or
 sunflower oil
1 medium onion, peeled and finely
 chopped
2.5cm/1" piece fresh root ginger, peeled
 and grated or finely chopped
1 tsp garam masala
1 tsp cumin seeds
1 tsp coriander seeds, crushed
1 tsp green cardamom pods, seeds
 removed and crushed
1 medium carrot, scrubbed and diced
400g/1 x 14oz can peeled Italian tomatoes
50g/2oz mushrooms, cleaned and finely
 chopped
1 tbsp shoyu sauce (Japanese soy sauce)
1 tbsp cider vinegar
Salt and freshly ground black pepper to
 taste
Freshly chopped parsley or coriander to
 garnish

1. Pick over the lentils and wash thoroughly.

2. Place in a large, thick-bottomed saucepan, cover with water or stock and bring to the boil. Turn off the heat, cover and leave to begin to swell.

3. Meanwhile, heat the margarine or oil in a separate saucepan and gently fry the onion, ginger and spices until they are well combined, softening and giving off a tempting aroma.

4. Add to the lentils, bring to the boil and start to add the other vegetables, allowing several minutes between each addition, beginning with the carrot followed by the tomatoes and lastly the chopped mushrooms.

5. Stir frequently to prevent sticking and check on liquid quantity regularly, adding more water or stock as necessary.

6. Just before the end of the cooking time – approximately 25 minutes depending on the age of the lentils – add the shoyu, cider vinegar and salt and pepper.

7. Cook for a few more minutes and serve hot garnished with slices of lemon and freshly chopped parsley or coriander.

TIME: Preparation takes about 25 minutes, cooking takes about 45 minutes.

SERVING IDEA: Serve with boiled wholegrain rice or jacket potatoes and salad made from beansprouts, red and green peppers and grated daikon.

VARIATION: Black olives can replace the chopped parsley or coriander.

LENTIL SAVOURY

This dish is quick and easy to prepare and very nutritious.

SERVES 4

175g/6oz lentils
½ tsp basil
½ tsp mixed herbs
2 medium onions, chopped
50g/2oz margarine
2 tbsps tomato purée
400g/1 x 14oz tin tomatoes
1 tsp brown sugar
Salt and black pepper
175g/6oz sliced Cheddar cheese
140ml/¼ pint soured cream

1. Soak the lentils overnight.

2. Add the herbs and simmer with the lentils in the cooking water until tender.

3. Sauté the onion in the fat until soft. Add the lentils and all the other ingredients apart from cheese and cream.

4. Simmer for 15 minutes until thickened and pour into a greased ovenproof dish.

5. Cover with the cheese and cream and grill or bake at 180°C/375°F/Gas Mark 4 until the cheese has melted.

TIME: Preparation takes 15 minutes, cooking takes 35-45 minutes.

COOK'S TIP: The soured cream can be served separately if desired.

SERVING IDEA: Serve hot with a mixed salad.

FREEZING: This lentil savoury will freeze well but do not cover it with cream and cheese until you are reheating it.

PIPER'S PIE

*Accompany this attractive dish with carrots
and sweetcorn for the perfect family meal.*

SERVES 4

450g/1lb potatoes, peeled and diced
175g/6oz mung beans
225g/8oz leeks
1 onion, sliced
½ tsp dill
2.5cm/1" fresh ginger, chopped or finely
  grated
1 tbsp concentrated apple juice
1 tsp miso

1. Boil the potatoes and mash with a little butter and seasoning.

2. In a separate pan, cover the mung beans with water and boil for 15-20 minutes until soft.

3. Meanwhile, generously butter an ovenproof casserole dish and put in the leeks, onion, dill, ginger and concentrated apple juice. Mix well.

4. Drain the beans, reserving the stock, and add to the casserole dish.

5. Dissolve the miso in a little of the bean stock and mix into the casserole which should be moist but not too wet.

6. Cover and cook at 200°C/400°F/Gas Mark 6 for 30-45 minutes, stirring a couple of times during the cooking and adding a little more bean stock if necessary.

7. Remove from the oven and cover with a layer of mashed potatoes.

8. Return to the oven to brown or brown under the grill.

TIME: Preparation takes 20 minutes, cooking takes 50-60 minutes.

VARIATION: A small tin of sweetcorn may be added to the pie before covering with the mashed potatoes.

RED BEAN STEW WITH CHILLI SAUCE

For convenience and speed tinned kidney beans can be used in this recipe.

SERVES 4

175g/6oz dried red kidney beans, soaked
  overnight
2 tbsps oil
1 large onion, chopped
1 clove garlic, crushed
400g/1 x 14oz tin tomatoes
½ tsp dried oregano
½ tsp dried basil
½ tsp shoyu sauce (Japanese soy sauce)
450g/1lb potatoes, peeled and diced
Salt and pepper

Chilli Sauce
25g/1oz butter or margarine
1 small clove garlic, crushed
1 small onion, grated
¾ tsp chilli powder
1 tbsp cider vinegar
75ml/3fl.oz bean stock or water
A little salt
1 tsp tomato purée
1 tbsp fresh coriander, finely chopped
1 tsp natural yogurt

1. Drain the beans, put into a large pan and cover with water. Boil vigorously for 10-15 minutes, turn down the heat and cook for about an hour until the beans are tender but still whole.

2. Heat the oil and fry the onion and garlic until soft.

3. Add the tomatoes, oregano, basil, shoyu and potatoes, cover and cook for 20 minutes until the potatoes are softened. Season to taste.

4. Drain the beans, reserving a little stock, and add to the onion and tomato mixture.

5. Cook gently for 5-10 minutes.

6. In a separate pan, melt the butter or margarine and cook the garlic and onion until soft.

7. Add the chilli powder and cook for a further 1-2 minutes.

8. Add the vinegar, stock, salt, tomato purée and coriander and cook for 5 minutes.

9. Remove from the heat and leave to cool slightly before stirring in the yogurt.

10. Serve with the sauce handed round separately.

TIME: Preparation takes 20 minutes. Cooking time, including the beans, 1 hour 35 minutes.

BEANY LASAGNE

*This tasty lasagne is suitable for a family
meal or entertaining friends.*

SERVES 4-6

8 strips wholewheat lasagne
1 large onion, peeled and finely chopped
1 tbsp vegetable oil
1-2 cloves garlic, crushed
225g/8oz cooked aduki beans
1 green pepper, de-seeded and chopped
400g/1 x 14oz can chopped tomatoes
1 tbsp tomato puree
1 tsp dried basil
1 tsp dried oregano
Shoyu sauce (Japanese soy sauce) or salt
Freshly ground black pepper

Sauce
25g/1oz margarine or butter
25g/1oz plain wholewheat flour
400ml/¾ pint dairy or soya milk
50g/2oz Cheddar cheese, grated (optional)
Salt
Freshly ground black pepper

1. Cook the lasagne in a large pan of boiling, salted water for 8-10 minutes until "al-dente". Drain well and drape over a cooling rack or the sides of a colander to cool and prevent sticking together.

2. Soften the onion in a little oil, sprinkling with a little salt to draw out the juice. Add the crushed garlic.

3. Add the beans, green pepper, chopped tomatoes, tomato puree and herbs.

4. Simmer for about 10 minutes or until the vegetables are tender.

5. Add shoyu sauce and season to taste.

6. To make the sauce, combine the margarine, flour and cold milk. Gradually bring to the boil, stirring continuously.

7. When thickened, allow to simmer, partly covered, for approximately 6 minutes.

8. Stir the cheese into the sauce and season.

9. Layer the lasagne in a greased dish in the following order: half the bean mix, half the pasta, rest of the bean mix, rest of the pasta, and top with the cheese sauce.

10. Bake at 180°C/350°F/Gas Mark 4 for 35 minutes or until golden brown and bubbling.

11. Serve in the dish in which it has been cooked.

TIME: Preparation takes 20 minutes, cooking takes about 60 minutes.

SERVING IDEA: Serve with a green salad.

COOK'S TIP: Pre-cooked lasagne can be used but it is important to add an extra amount of liquid to the dish in order to allow the pasta to absorb enough fluid while cooking.

SWEET BEAN CURRY

This excellent curry will freeze well for up to six weeks.

SERVES 4

175g/6oz red kidney beans, soaked
   overnight
25g/1oz butter or margarine
1 onion, sliced
1 apple, cored and chopped
175g/6oz mushrooms, sliced
1 tbsp curry powder
25g/1oz unbleached flour
570ml/1 pint bean stock or bean stock
   and water
Salt to taste
1 tbsp lemon juice
1 tbsp chutney
50g/2oz sultanas
50g/2oz coconut cream, grated or
   chopped

1. Drain the beans, put into a large pan and cover with cold water.

2. Bring to the boil and boil vigorously for 10-15 minutes, turn down the heat and boil for about an hour until the beans are tender but still whole.

3. Melt the butter or margarine and cook the onion until it is very brown.

4. Add the apple and mushrooms and cook for 2-3 minutes.

5. Add the curry powder and flour and cook for a couple of minutes, stirring all the time.

6. Gradually add the bean stock and stir until smooth.

7. Add the seasoning, lemon juice, chutney, sultanas and beans and cook for 10-15 minutes.

8. Just before serving add the coconut cream and stir until dissolved.

TIME: Preparation takes 25 minutes. Cooking time, including the beans, 1 hour 25 minutes.

SERVING IDEA: Serve with boiled brown rice and fried plantains – peel, cut into 1.2cm slices and fry in hot oil until golden brown. If unavailable you can use unripe green bananas. Garnish the curry with quarters of hard-boiled eggs.

MUESLI DE-LUXE

*Dried mixed fruit and organic muesli base can
be purchased at most wholefood stores and health
food shops or you can mix your own if preferred.*

MAKES 1.6KG/3½ lbs

450g/1lb dried mixed fruit (apples, pears,
    apricots, prunes)
450g/1lb organic muesli base
    (wheatflakes, porridge oats, rye flakes,
    pearl barley flakes, jumbo oat flakes)
50g/2oz wheatgerm
100g/4oz sunflower seeds
175g/6oz sultanas
175g/6oz lexia raisins
100g/4oz hazel nuts
100g/4oz brazil nuts, halved

1. Chop the dried mixed fruit into small pieces with a pair of kitchen scissors.

2. Place in a mixing bowl with all the other ingredients.

3. Mix well.

4. Store in an airtight container in a cool place.

TIME: Preparation takes 10 minutes.

SERVING IDEA: Serve for breakfast with milk, soya milk, yogurt or fruit juice and add fresh fruit whenever possible or simmer with milk, water or fruit juice for 5 minutes and eat hot. Muesli can be used as a base for biscuits and a topping for fruit crumbles.

VARIATION: The nuts can be varied according to taste and pumpkin seeds can be added.

247

GRANOLA

Serve for breakfast with milk, soya milk, fruit juices or yogurt.

MAKES 1.5KG/3¼ lbs

450g/1lb organic muesli base
    (wheatflakes, porridge oats, rye flakes,
    pearl barley flakes, jumbo oat flakes)
100g/4oz sunflower seeds
50g/2oz wheatgerm
100g/4oz sesame seeds
75g/3oz soya flour
50g/2oz dried skimmed milk powder
50g/2oz desiccated coconut
100g/4oz chopped mixed nuts
175ml/6fl.oz sunflower or safflower oil
175ml/6fl.oz clear honey
175g/6oz sultanas

1. Put all the ingredients apart from the sultanas into a large mixing bowl.

2. Stir with a wooden spoon until all the dry ingredients are coated with the oil and honey.

3. Spread the mixture evenly over 2 large baking trays.

4. Bake at 150°C/300°F/Gas Mark 2 for about 1 hour stirring frequently until the mixture is golden brown.

5. Remove from the oven and allow to cool on the trays.

6. Add the sultanas and mix well.

7. Place in an airtight container and store in a cool place.

TIME: Preparation takes 10 minutes, cooking takes 1 hour.

COOK'S TIP: Organic muesli base and chopped mixed nuts can be purchased at most wholefood stores and health food shops.

VARIATION: To vary the flavour, use malt extract in place of honey – this may need to be heated slightly before incorporating it into the Granola.

BUTTER BEAN ONE-POT

This is a quick to make, all-in-one supper dish.

SERVES 4

2 tbsps vegetable oil
1 green pepper, finely chopped
1 large onion, finely chopped
2 sticks celery, diced
400g/1 x 14oz tin tomatoes
2 large potatoes, peeled and diced
280ml/½ pint vegetable stock or water
2 tbsps finely chopped parsley
Salt and pepper
450g/1lb cooked butter beans

1. Put the oil, pepper, onion and celery into a pan and cook gently until the onion begins to brown.

2. Add the tomatoes and their juice, plus the potatoes, stock, parsley, salt and pepper.

3. Simmer for about 30 minutes or until the liquid is reduced by half.

4. Add the beans and heat through gently for 5-10 minutes.

TIME: Preparation takes about 15 minutes, cooking takes 50 minutes.

SERVING IDEA: Serve with lots of crusty bread. Garlic bread also goes well with this dish.

VARIATION: To make a more substantial main course dish, follow the recipe to the end of instruction 3. Add the beans and stir well. Place in a casserole dish, top with a crumble mixture and bake in a hot oven for 25 minutes.

BUTTER BEANS IN TOMATO SAUCE

*A tasty tomato sauce perfectly complements
the beans in this easy recipe.*

SERVES 4-6

175g/6oz butter beans, soaked overnight
50g/2oz vegetable fat
1 onion, sliced
6 medium tomatoes, sliced
50g/2oz flour
1 bay leaf
A little milk
Salt and pepper
Chopped parsley

1. Drain the butter beans and put into a pan with fresh water to cover, cook slowly until soft.

2. Melt the fat and cook the onions with the tomatoes and bay leaf until soft.

3. Stir in the flour, and add a little cooking water from the beans to make a thick sauce.

4. Stir well and add a little milk and seasoning to taste.

5. Remove the bay leaf and pour the sauce over the beans.

6. Sprinkle with the chopped parsley.

TIME: Preparation takes 20 minutes. Cooking time, including the beans, 1½ -1¾ hours.

SERVING IDEA: Serve with baked potatoes and lightly cooked vegetables.

COOK'S TIP: When cold, this savoury can be mashed to make a sandwich paste or for use with a mixed salad. Any leftovers can be used as a basis for soup.

COOKING FOR SPECIAL OCCASIONS

How often have you heard the phrase 'Oh, it's nothing, I just threw it together at the last minute'? There are, however, few people who can say this in all truth. For the most part, a good host or hostess will have spent half the time on the planning, one quarter of the time on the shopping and the remaining time on the actual cooking. From a dinner party to a picnic, a buffet to a barbecue, the secret is forward planning.

Make lists – they are invaluable, not only for shopping but for all the steps you must take to the big event. There is nothing more frustrating than to be serving the starter only to realise you haven't put the vegetables on to cook. When selecting your menu, try to choose dishes that can be prepared in advance. You owe it to yourself to enjoy the occasion and your guests will not expect you to be slaving away in the kitchen for long periods before and during the meal. If you are not very experienced, try to choose two courses that do not require last minute attention: a pre-prepared soup and a cold dessert will give plenty of time to concentrate on the main course.

This chapter features a variety of dishes that are appropriate for occasions such as dinner parties, intimate meals and Christmas dinner. So no matter what the event you will never again have to worry about what to serve your guests.

CELERY STUFFED WITH SMOKED TOFU PATÉ

*These tasty nibbles are perfect for drinks
parties, picnics and buffets.*

50g/2oz hard vegetarian margarine
1 medium onion, chopped
1 clove garlic, chopped
½ bunch watercress, roughly chopped
75g/3oz smoked tofu
50g/2oz Cheddar cheese, grated
1 head celery
A little parpika

---

1. Melt the margarine and fry the onion and garlic until soft.

2. Add the watercress and stir for 15 seconds until it becomes limp.

3. Place in a liquidiser with the rest of the ingredients, excluding the celery and paprika.

4. Liquidise until smooth, pushing down with a wooden spoon if necessary.

5. Leave to cool.

6. Clean the celery, stuff with the paté and sprinkle with a little paprika.

7. Refrigerate for at least 2 hours before serving.

TIME: Preparation and cooking takes about 15 minutes.

VARIATION: Serve with twist of lemon and very thin brown bread and butter.

FREEZING: This paté freezes well for up to 6 weeks. Thaw at room temperature for 2 hours or overnight in the refrigerator.

BRAZILIAN AVOCADOS

*The perfect way to impress your dinner guests
right from the first course.*

SERVES 4

2 large ripe avocados
A little lemon juice
Salt and pepper
50g/2oz finely chopped Brazil nuts
50g/2oz Cheddar cheese, grated
2 tbsps Parmesan cheese
2 level tbsps freshly chopped parsley
2 firm ripe tomatoes, skinned and finely
    chopped
Wholemeal breadcrumbs
25g/1oz melted butter
A little paprika

1. Halve the avocados and carefully remove the flesh from the skins. Brush the inside of the skins with a little of the lemon juice.

2. Dice the avocado and put into a bowl with a sprinkling of lemon juice and the seasoning.

3. Add the nuts, cheeses, parsley and tomato.

4. Mix gently.

5. Spoon the filling into the avocado shells, sprinkle with the breadcrumbs and drizzle the butter over the top.

6. Dust with the paprika and bake at 200°C/400°F/Gas Mark 6 for 15 minutes.

TIME: Preparation takes about 10 minutes, cooking takes 15 minutes.

COOK'S TIP: Do not prepare this dish too far in advance as the avocado may discolour.

SERVING IDEA: Serve with a little salad as a starter or with baked potatoes, vegetables and tossed salad for a main course.

INDONESIAN-STYLE STUFFED PEPPERS

*For this adaptable recipe you can substitute
pine nuts or peanuts if you don't have cashews.*

SERVES 8 AS A STARTER

30ml/2 tbsps olive oil
1 medium onion, peeled and chopped
1 clove garlic, crushed
2 tsps turmeric
1 tsp crushed coriander seed
2 tbsps dessicated coconut
100g/4oz mushrooms, chopped
75g/3oz bulgar wheat
50g/2oz raisins
25g/1oz creamed coconut
280ml/½ pint stock or water
200g/7oz tomatoes, skinned and chopped
50g/2oz cashew nuts
4 small green peppers, de-seeded and cut
   in half lenthways
2 tsps lemon juice
Stock for cooking

1. Heat the oil and fry the onion and garlic until lightly browned.

2. Add the turmeric, coriander and dessicated coconut and cook gently for about 2 minutes.

3. Add the mushrooms and bulgar wheat and cook for a further 2 minutes.

4. Add the rest of the ingredients except the nuts, lemon juice, peppers, and cooking stock, and simmer gently for 15-20 minutes until the bulgar wheat is cooked.

5. Toast the cashew nuts in a dry frying pan until golden brown.

6. Blanch the peppers in boiling water for 3 minutes.

7. Mix the nuts and lemon juice with the rest of the ingredients and fill the peppers with the mixture.

8. Place the filled peppers on the bottom of a large casserole dish and pour stock around the peppers.

9. Cook 180°C/350°F/Gas Mark 4 for 20 minutes.

10. Drain peppers and place on a hot plate to serve.

TIME: Preparation takes 20 minutes, cooking takes 45 minutes.

FREEZING: The cooked peppers will freeze well for up to 3 months.

COURGETTE AND PINE NUT LASAGNE WITH AUBERGINE SAUCE

*This unusual lasagne will leave your guests guessing as
to the delicious combination of ingredients.*

SERVES 4

12 strips of wholewheat lasagne
75g/3oz pine nuts
25g/1oz butter
675g/1½lbs courgettes, trimmed and
    sliced
275g/10oz ricotta cheese
½ tsp grated nutmeg
1 tbsp olive oil
1 large aubergine, sliced
140ml/5fl.oz water
2 tsps shoyu sauce (Japanese soy sauce)
75g/3oz Cheddar cheese, grated

1. Place the lasagne in a large roasting tin and completely cover with boiling water. Leave for 10 minutes and then drain.

2. Place the pine nuts in a dry pan and roast gently for 2 minutes. Set aside.

3. Melt the butter and cook the courgettes with a little water until just tender.

4. Combine the courgettes, pine nuts and ricotta cheese.

5. Add the nutmeg and mix together thoroughly.

6. In a separate pan, heat the olive oil and sauté the aubergine for 4 minutes.

7. Add the water and shoyu and simmer, covered, until soft.

8. Liquidise, adding a little extra water if necessary.

9. Place 4 strips of lasagne on the bottom of a greased 3 pint rectangular dish and top with half the courgette mixture.

10. Place 4 more strips of lasagne over the courgettes and add half the aubergine sauce followed by the rest of the courgettes.

11. Cover with the remaining lasagne and the rest of the sauce.

12. Sprinkle the grated cheese over the top and bake for 40 minutes at 190°C/375°F/Gas Mark 5, until the cheese is golden brown.

TIME: Preparation takes about 30 minutes, cooking takes 50 minutes.

SERVING IDEA: Serve with a crunchy mixed salad and Creamy Jacket Potatoes – bake the potatoes until soft, remove the potato from the skins and mash with a little milk, butter and seasoning. Cool a little and place the mixture in a piping bag with a large nozzle. Pipe the mixture back into the potato shells and re-heat when required. Note: you will need to cook a couple of extra potatoes in order to have plenty of filling when they are mashed.

PARSNIP ROAST

*This colourful roast is perfect for picnics
as well as entertaining.*

SERVES 4

450g/1lb parsnips
1 tbsp freshly chopped tarragon
1 small onion, very finely chopped
2 eggs, beaten
Salt
Black pepper

1. Line and grease a 450g/1lb loaf tin.

2. Peel and slice the parsnips, cover with water and cook until soft.

3. Drain the parsnips, dry off over a low heat and mash well with a potato masher or fork.

4. Add the tarragon, onion, eggs and seasoning and mix together well.

5. Put the mixture into the loaf tin and smooth over the top with a knife.

6. Cover with foil and bake at 170°C/ 325°F/Gas Mark 3 for 1 hour.

TIME: Preparation takes 10 minutes, cooking takes about 1 hour.

SERVING IDEA: Garnish with fresh tarragon and slices of green pepper. Serve hot with a platter of mixed cooked vegetables – carrot sticks, cauliflower florets and sliced red and green peppers – or cold on a bed of lollo rosso or oak leaf lettuce with a carrot coleslaw.

VARIATION: Use 2 tbsps of chopped parsley if tarragon is not available.

COOK'S TIP: This loaf can be assembled earlier in the day and refrigerated until just before cooking.

ASPARAGUS AND OLIVE QUICHE

*An interesting combination which gives
a new twist to a classic dish.*

MAKES 2 x 10" QUICHES

2 x 25.4cm/10" part baked pastry shells
6 eggs
570ml/1 pint single cream
1 tsp salt
Pinch of nutmeg
Salt and pepper
2 tbsps flour
2 cans green asparagus tips
175g/6oz green olives
2 onions, finely chopped and sautéed in a
    little butter until soft
75g/3oz Cheddar cheese, grated
2 tbsps Parmesan cheese
50g/2oz butter

1. Whisk the eggs with the cream.

2. Add the salt, nutmeg and seasoning.

3. Mix a little of the mixture with the flour until smooth, then add to the cream mixture.

4. Arrange the asparagus tips, olives and onion in the pastry shells and pour the cream mixture over the top.

5. Sprinkle with the grated Cheddar and Parmesan.

6. Dot with the butter and bake at 190°C/375°F/Gas Mark 5 for 25 minutes.

7. Turn down the oven to 180°C/350°F/Gas Mark 4 for a further 15 minutes until the quiches are golden.

T IME: Preparation takes 20 minutes, cooking takes 40 minutes.

F REEZING: The quiches may be frozen but a slightly better result is obtained if you freeze the pastry shells and add the filling just before baking.

SRI LANKAN RICE

*Serve this rice hot as an accompaniment
to vegetable curries or dhal.*

SERVES 12

3 tbsps sunflower oil
1 medium onion, finely chopped
2 cloves garlic, crushed
1 heaped tsp ground cumin
1 heaped tsp ground coriander
1 heaped tsp paprika
1 level dstsp turmeric
¼ tsp chilli or cayenne pepper
150g/5oz Basmati rice, washed and
    drained
325ml/12fl.oz skimmed milk
1 tsp salt
Ground pepper to taste
225g/8oz mange tout, topped, tailed and
    cut in half
100g/4oz mushrooms, washed and sliced
1 small tin (5oz) sweetcorn, drained
50g/2oz sultanas, washed and soaked

1. Heat the oil in a large non-stick pan.

2. Gently fry the onion and garlic for 4-5 minutes.

3. Add the cumin, coriander, paprika, turmeric and chilli, and fry for a further 3-4 minutes – do not allow the mixture to burn.

4. Add the washed rice and mix well with the onions and spices for about 2 minutes.

5. Add the milk, salt and pepper, stir gently, bring to the boil, cover and simmer until all the liquid is absorbed and the rice is cooked – approximately 15-20 minutes.

6. Whilst the rice is cooking, steam the mange tout, mushrooms, sweetcorn and sultanas and fold into the rice.

8. Cool and turn out onto a serving dish.

TIME: Preparation takes 15 minutes, cooking takes 25-30 minutes.

SERVING IDEA: Sprinkle with 2 tbsps of freshly chopped coriander
or parsley if not available.

VARIATION: Other lightly steamed vegetables may be used according to season and
personal taste – broccoli florets, diced carrots, peas and sliced green peppers.

FESTIVE ROAST

Never again will Christmas dinner be a
problem with this festive roast.

SERVES 8

2 tbsps sunflower oil
2 medium onions, finely chopped
2 cloves garlic, crushed
450g/1lb finely ground cashew nuts
225g/8oz wholemeal breadcrumbs
2 beaten eggs or 4 tbsps soya flour mixed
   with a little water
1 heaped tsp mixed herbs
2 tsps Marmite or yeast extract
280ml/½ pint boiling water
Salt and pepper

1. Heat the oil and fry the onion and garlic until soft.

2. Place the onions and garlic into a large bowl. Add all the other ingredients and mix well.

3. Butter or line a 2lb loaf tin and spoon in the mixture.

4. Cover with a double thickness of foil and cook in the oven at 180°C/350°F/Gas Mark 4 for about 1 hour 20 minutes until firm.

5. Allow to cool for about 10 minutes in the tin before turning out.

TIME: Preparation takes about 15 minutes, cooking takes about 1 hour 20 minutes.

FREEZING: An excellent dish to freeze cooked or uncooked, although a slightly better result is obtained if frozen uncooked and thawed overnight in the refrigerator.

SERVING IDEA: Serve with a wine sauce or gravy and decorate with sprigs of holly.

CARROT AND PARSNIP MEDLEY

The perfect accompaniment to Festive Roast.

SERVES 8

75g/3oz butter
8 medium carrots, peeled and sliced
4 parsnips, peeled and cut into rings
1 level tsp ground ginger
½ tsp grated nutmeg
Salt and pepper
Juice of 1 lemon
2 tsps fine sugar
Chopped parsley

1. Melt the butter in a large pan and add the carrots and parsnips.

2. Sauté very gently for 2-3 minutes then add the ginger, nutmeg, seasoning, lemon juice and enough water to cover the vegetables.

3. Cover and simmer for 15-20 minutes until the vegetables are soft and the liquid has evaporated.

4. Add the sugar and increase the heat, tossing the vegetables until they are glossy.

5. Transfer to a heated serving dish and sprinkle with the chopped parsley.

TIME: Preparation takes 10 minutes, cooking takes 20-25 minutes.

VARIATION: Any chopped fresh herbs may be used for garnishing – coriander is a good alternative.

COOK'S TIP: Lemons yield more juice if you first roll them backwards and forwards on a kitchen work surface with your hands using medium pressure.

MINCE PIES

*Ordinary mincemeat usually contains suet
so buy the vegetarian kind.*

MAKES ABOUT 16

225g/8oz wholewheat self-raising flour
Pinch of salt
100g/4oz margarine or butter
75g/3oz brown sugar, crushed or finely
   ground
Yolk of 1 egg
30ml/2 tbsps cold water
175-225g/6-8oz vegetarian mincemeat
A little milk

1. Combine the flour and salt. Lightly rub in the margarine or butter until the mixture resembles fine breadcrumbs. Mix in the sugar.

2. Beat the egg yolk and water together and add to the flour mixture, mixing until a ball of dough is formed.

3. Wrap in greaseproof paper or cling film and refrigerate for at least half an hour.

4. Roll out the pastry using lots of flour, to about 0.5cm/¼" thick and cut out fifteen 8cm/3" rounds for the bases and fifteen 6.5cm/2" rounds for the lids.

5. Grease 6cm/2½" patty tins and line with the larger rounds. Half fill with mincemeat and cover with the lids, pressing lightly round the edges. Brush with milk.

6. Bake in a preheated oven 200°C/400°F/Gas Mark 6 for 20 minutes or until the pies are golden brown.

TIME: Preparation takes about 35 minutes, cooking takes 20-25 minutes.

FREEZING: The mince pies can be made well in advance and frozen for up to 3 months.

COOK'S TIP: Crush the brown sugar between sheets of greaseproof paper with a rolling pin if you do not have a grinder.

TOFU SPINACH FLAN

Serve this tasty flan with a medley of
lightly cooked fresh vegetables.

SERVES 4

Pastry
1 tsp brown sugar
2-3 tbsps water
2 tsps oil
100g/4oz wholemeal flour
½ tsp baking powder
Pinch of salt
50g/2oz Granose or other hard
   margarine

Filling
225g/8oz spinach
275g/10oz tofu
Juice of 1 lemon
2 tbsps shoyu sauce (Japanese soy sauce)
4 tbsps sunflower oil
140ml/¼ pint soya milk
Salt according to taste
175g/6oz onions, chopped

1. Dissolve the sugar in the water and mix in the oil. Keep cool.

2. Mix the flour, baking powder and salt together in a large bowl.

3. Rub in the margarine until the mixture resembles fine breadcrumbs.

4. Add the fluid mixture and mix into the flour, using more water if necessary. The dough should be of a wettish consistency.

5. Leave to rest under the upturned bowl for half an hour.

6. Preheat the oven to 190°C/375°F/Gas Mark 5.

7. Roll out the dough to line an 18-20cm/ 7-8" flan dish.

8. Pinch the base all over and bake blind for 5-6 minutes.

9. Wash the spinach, drain and cook in it's own juices in a covered pan until soft – about 5-8 minutes.

10. Drain the spinach, chop and set aside.

11. Crumble the tofu into a blender, add the lemon juice, shoyu, 2 tbsps of the oil, the soya milk and salt. Blend to a thick creamy consistency. Adjust the seasoning if necessary.

12. Chop the onions and fry them in the remaining oil until lightly browned.

13. Add the spinach and fold in the tofu cream.

14. Pour the mixture into the prepared flan shell and bake in the middle of the oven for 30 minutes or until set.

15. Allow to cool for about 10 minutes before serving.

TIME: Preparation takes 25 minutes, cooking takes 45 minutes.

WATCHPOINT: The filling may develop 'cracks' on cooling but this is normal.

CHRISTMAS PUDDING

A traditional end to a traditional meal.

SERVES 8

100g/4oz wholewheat self-raising flour
225g/8oz vegetarian suet
Grated rind of one small lemon
½ tsp grated nutmeg
100g/4oz sultanas
225g/8oz raisins
100g/4oz candied peel
25g/1oz chopped almonds
2 eggs, beaten
2 tbsps clear honey
140ml/¼ pint milk

---

1. Combine the flour and suet, add the lemon rind, nutmeg, fruit, peel and almonds.

2. Beat the eggs and whisk together with the honey.

3. Add to the dry ingredients with the milk and mix well.

4. Put into a greased pudding basin and cover with greaseproof paper.

5. Place the pudding basin in a saucepan with about 1" of boiling water and steam for 3 hours, topping up with more water as required.

6. Cool and wrap well in a clean tea towel. Store for between 4-6 weeks.

7. On the day on which the pudding is to be eaten, steam for a further 1½ hours before serving.

TIME: Preparation takes 40 minutes. Cooking takes 3 hours plus 1½ hours on the day of serving.

SERVING IDEA: Serve with rum butter, a white sauce or coconut cream.

CELEBRATION PUDDING

*This makes a delicious alternative to the
traditional Christmas Pudding and can be
made for any celebration dinner.*

SERVES 8

First layer
175g/6oz sultanas
175g/6oz raisins
100g/4oz dates
2 tbsps concentrated apple juice
280ml/½ pint fresh orange juice
Juice of ½ lemon
¼ tsp grated nutmeg
2 tbsps rum or brandy
50g/2oz chopped almonds

Second layer
225g/8oz dried apricots
280ml/½ pint fresh orange juice
Juice of ½ lemon
2.5cm/1" stick of cinnamon
50g/2oz ground almonds

Third layer
280ml/½ pint whipped cream
1 tbsp brandy (optional)

1. For the first layer, soak the sultanas, raisins and dates in orange and lemon juice for 2 hours.

2. For the second layer, soak the apricots in the orange and lemon juice for 2 hours.

3. Simmer the apricots and fruit juice with the cinnamon stick for about 40 minutes or until the apricots are soft.

4. Remove the cinnamon stick, beat the apricots to a purée and stir in the ground almonds.

5. Simmer the sultanas, raisins and dates in the apple juice, orange juice, lemon juice and nutmeg for about 40 minutes or until thick and syrupy.

6. Stir in the rum or brandy and the chopped almonds.

7. Stir the brandy into the whipped cream for the third layer.

8. Line a round pudding basin with cling film and build the pudding up in layers beginning with the sultana and raisin mixture followed by the apricot mixture and lastly the whipped cream, making sure you end with a layer of the dark mixture on the top.

9. Cover and chill well.

10. Turn out onto a serving dish, remove the cling film and flame before serving.

TIME: Preparation takes 10 minutes, soaking takes 2 hours and cooking takes 40 minutes.

FREEZING: Freeze in the pudding basin for up to a month. Thaw at room temperature for 6 hours.

CHRISTMAS CAKE

*This rich, moist fruit cake is made without sugar
or eggs and is suitable for vegans.*

100ml/4fl.oz clear honey
175ml/6fl.oz safflower or sunflower oil
75g/3oz soya flour
280ml/½ pint water
15ml/1 tbsp rum or 1 tsp rum essence
Grated rind and juice of 1 orange
Grated rind and juice of 1 lemon
50g/2oz flaked almonds
75g/3oz dried figs, chopped
75g/3oz dried dates, chopped
50g/2oz dried apricots, chopped
225g/8oz wholewheat self-raising flour
Pinch salt
2 level tsps mixed spice
225g/8oz currants
225g/8oz sultanas
225g/8oz raisins

1. Assemble all the ingredients and preheat the oven to 170°C/325°F/Gas Mark 3. Line a 23cm/9" square cake tin with greaseproof paper.

2. Cream the honey and the oil together.

3. Mix the soya flour with the water and gradually add to the oil and honey mixture, beating well.

4. Beat in the rum and the grated rind and juice of the orange and lemon. Add the almonds, figs, dates and apricots.

5. Mix the flour with the salt and spice and mix together the currants, sultanas and raisins.

6. Stir half the flour and half the currant mixture into the soya cream, then stir in the remainder. Spoon into the prepared tin.

7. Cover with two or three layers of brown paper and bake for 3¼ to 3½ hours, or until a skewer inserted into the centre comes out clean.

8. Cool for 10 minutes and turn out onto a wire rack to cool.

9. Keep in an airtight tin.

TIME: Preparation takes about 40 minutes, cooking takes 3¼ to 3½ hours.

COOK'S TIP: This cake will keep well but is best made three to four weeks before cutting and stored, wrapped in foil or greaseproof paper, in an airtight tin.

SERVING IDEA: Leave plain or decorate with glazed fruits. Try serving the Yorkshire way with chunks of sharp vegetarian cheese.

VARIATION: Other dried fruits may be used instead of figs, dates and apricots but make sure that the overall measurements stay the same.

STRAWBERRY AND BANANA FROST

*This speedy dessert can be started ahead of
time and completed just before serving.*

SERVES 4-6

450g/1lb strawberries
1 large banana
175ml/6fl.oz fromage frais
Few drops vanilla essence
1 tsp clear honey

1. Wash and hull the strawberries and put half of them in the refrigerator.

2. Peel the banana and cut into pieces.

3. Cut the remaining strawberries in halves, quarters if they are large, and freeze with the banana until solid.

4. Just before serving, remove the strawberries and banana from the freezer.

5. Place the frozen strawberries, banana, fromage frais, vanilla essence and honey in a food processor or liquidiser and process until smooth. You will need to push the mixture down two or three times with a spatula or wooden spoon.

6. Divide the mixture between 4 or 6 individual serving dishes and place the remaining strawberries around the 'frost' mixture.

7. Serve at once.

TIME: Preparation takes 10 minutes, freezing takes at least 1 hour.

VARIATION: Pineapple, raspberries or apple can be substituted for the above.

NOTE: For a creamier 'frost' try Greek yogurt instead of fromage frais but this will add a few extra calories.

HAWAIIAN PINEAPPLE PANCAKES

*You can try many different fruits as a
filling for these delicious pancakes.*

MAKES 12 PANCAKES

175g/6oz flour
Pinch salt
2 small eggs, beaten
450ml/¾ pint milk
1 tsp vegetable oil
2 tbsps cold water
Oil for frying

Filling
1 x 450g/15oz can pineapple
225g/8oz cottage cheese
25-50g/1-2oz sugar, finely ground

1. Sift the flour and salt into a bowl.

2. Make a well in the centre and add the beaten eggs.

3. Gradually beat in half the milk and mix until smooth.

4. Stir in the rest of the milk, the oil and the cold water.

5. Refrigerate for at least 1 hour.

6. Place a little oil into a 15cm/6" frying pan and heat until just smoking, pour in 2 tbsps of the batter and swirl round until the bottom is evenly coated.

7. Cook until the underside is golden, flip over and repeat.

8. Cool on a wire rack.

9. Repeat this process until all the batter has been used.

10. The pancakes can be frozen at this stage and filled just before cooking by interleaving them with greaseproof paper and wrapping well with foil.

11. To make the filling, drain the pineapple and chop finely. Sieve the cottage cheese.

12. Mix the pineapple, cheese and sugar together. Divide equally between the pancakes and roll up around the filling.

13. Place in a single layer in an ovenproof dish. Cover with foil and freeze.

14. To serve, remove the wrapping and thaw at room temperature for 2-3 hours.

15. Reheat at 200°C/400°F/Gas mark 6 for 20 minutes until heated through.

TIME: Preparation takes 10 minutes, cooking takes about 40 minutes.

SERVING IDEA: Serve the pancakes garnished with hot pineapple rings.

BRANDIED ORANGES WITH PEACH AND MANGO CREAM

An attractive dessert which tastes as good as it looks.

SERVES 4

6 large jaffa oranges
3 tbsps brandy
2 mangoes, peeled and cut into chunks
4 small ripe peaches, peeled and roughly
　chopped
3 tbsps double cream

1. Finely pare the zest from 3 of the oranges and boil the zest in a little water for 2 minutes.

2. Remove and cool.

3. Peel the oranges using a sharp knife, making sure that all the pith is removed.

4. Slice thinly, arrange the slices in a serving dish and sprinkle the zest over the top.

5. Sprinkle the brandy over the top and refrigerate for about an hour.

6. Put the mangoes and peaches into a liquidiser and blend until smooth.

7. Stir in the cream and refrigerate until required.

8. Hand round the peach and mango cream when serving the oranges.

TIME: Preparation takes 20 minutes, cooking takes 2 minutes.

VARIATION: Greek yogurt may be used instead of double cream or it may be omitted altogether.

COOK'S TIP: Use a zester to remove the zest from the oranges.

CAROB SUNDAE

A delightful treat which provides the perfect end to any meal.

SERVES 4

Carob Dessert
225ml/8fl.oz milk or soya milk
1 tsp pure vanilla essence
1 tbsp sunflower oil
2 tbsps honey
¼ tsp sea salt
1 tbsp cornflour
¼ tsp Caro (coffee substitute)
1 tbsp carob powder

Vanilla Custard
1 tbsp cornmeal flour
100ml/4fl.oz milk or soya milk
1 tbsp honey
½ tsp pure vanilla essence

Filling
1 large banana, chopped
1 punnet of strawberries, hulled, washed
    and halved.

---

1. Blend all the carob dessert ingredients together in a saucepan and cook until thick, stirring continuously.

2. Leave to cool.

3. Mix the cornmeal flour with a little of the milk to make a smooth paste and add the honey and vanilla essence.

4. Heat the remaining milk until nearly boiling and pour over the cornmeal mixture, stirring until smooth.

5. Return to the pan and re-heat gently until thick, stirring constantly.

6. Leave to cool.

7. Add half the carob dessert to the chopped banana and mix together carefully.

8. Fill sundae glasses with layers of carob dessert, banana mixture, strawberries, vanilla custard and finally the plain carob dessert.

9. Chill before serving.

TIME: Preparation takes about 20 minutes, cooking takes 10 minutes.

SERVING IDEA: Serve decorated with dessicated coconut.

VARIATION: Raspberries can be used if strawberries are not available.

FRUIT FANTASIA

A pretty dessert which is simple to prepare and perfectly refreshing.

SERVES 8

1 melon
4 large grapefruit
100g/4oz black grapes
100g/4oz green grapes
2 red eating apples
1 small carton single cream
Mint leaves for garnishing

1. Cut the melon into quarters. Remove the flesh, cut into 1" pieces and place in a large bowl.

2. Make zig-zag cuts around each grapefruit, halve, remove the flesh and add to the melon, reserving the grapefruit shells.

3. Remove the seeds from the grapes and cut into halves.

4. Wash the apples and slice finely, leaving the skin on. Add to the grapefruit, grapes and melon.

5. Chill for at least an hour.

6. Mix the single cream carefully into the fruit and pile into the grapefruit shells.

7. Garnish with the mint before serving.

TIME: Preparation takes about 10 minutes, chilling takes at least one hour.

SERVING IDEA: Serve in individual dishes containing crushed ice and garnished with mint leaves.

VARIATION: If time is short use seedless grapes and leave whole.

DESSERTS

'The proof of the pudding is in the eating'.
Henry Glapthorne
The Hollander 1635

By far and away the easiest and healthiest dessert to serve is fresh fruit. A bowl filled with a wide selection of fruits in season provides a wonderful centrepiece for any dessert table. There are many occasions, however, when delicious home-made desserts cannot be beaten. Ice cream is one of the most popular and is well worth making in large quantities when fresh fruit is cheap and plentiful. There are also lots of alternatives to rich cholesterol-laded creams such as yogurt, and fromage frais.

If you are making a pie or pastry dish, it is just as easy to make two, three or even four and freeze them for a later date. Should unexpected guests turn up, everyday puddings can be transformed by the addition of a few chopped nuts and whipped cream piped around the dish. Serve light desserts at the end of a filling main meal and more substantial puddings such as cheesecake after a light meal or salad. If you are short of time don't forget that a mixed cheese platter is a very acceptable finale and you'll find a wide range of vegetarian cheeses are available at many supermarkets as well as specialist cheese shops.

Flambéed Caramel Custards

The perfect dinner party dessert.

SERVES 6

Caramel
50g/2oz soft brown sugar
2 tbsps water

Custards
3 eggs
100g/4oz finely ground soft brown sugar
420ml/¾ pint milk
A pinch mixed spice
Thinly pared rind of 1 orange
140ml/¼ pint Spanish brandy

1. Melt the sugar in the water over a moderate heat and boil until it begins to turn golden brown.

2. Remove from the heat and divide the mixture to coat the base of 6 ramekin dishes.

3. Whisk the eggs and add the sugar.

4. Put the milk into a saucepan with the spice and orange rind and heat until simmering.

5. Add to the eggs and mix well.

6. Pour equal quantities of custard in the ramekin dishes and place them in a deep roasting tin.

7. Pour in enough water to come up to about two thirds of the sides of the ramekin dishes.

8. Bake at 150°C/300°F/Gas Mark 2 for about 1 hour or until the custard has set.

9. Turn out onto a hot serving dish.

10. Heat the brandy in a ladle or small pan and ignite for about 10 seconds.

11. Pour over the custards and serve immediately.

TIME: Preparation takes 5 minutes, cooking takes about 1 hour.

WINDWARD FRUIT BASKET

An impressive dessert which is surprisingly easy to prepare.

SERVES 4-6

1 large ripe melon
2 apples
Juice of 1 lime
2 mangoes
2 kiwi fruit
450g/1lb strawberries
225g/½lb raspberries
3 tbsps honey
2 tbsps dark rum
50g/2oz butter

1. Cut the top off the melon and scoop out the seeds.

2. Using a melon baller, scoop out balls of melon and place in a large bowl.

3. Remove the core from the apples, dice and toss in the lime juice.

4. Peel and chop the mangoes.

5. Peel and slice the kiwi fruit.

6. Combine all the fruits.

7. Heat the honey, rum and butter gently until the butter has melted.

8. Cool, and pour over the fruits.

9. Toss gently and fill the melon shell with the fruit mixture.

10. Place on a serving dish and serve immediately.

TIME: Preparation takes 20 minutes, cooking takes 2 minutes.

SERVING IDEA: For a special occasion, make holes around the top of the melon with a skewer and decorated with fresh flowers.

VARIATION: Use any fresh fruits in season, pears, peaches etc.

STRAWBERRY SORBET

Serve at the end of a very rich meal or between the main course and dessert if serving a light summer dinner.

SERVES 4

1 medium lemon
280ml/½ pint water
175g/6oz sugar
675g/1½ lb strawberries
2 egg whites

1. Pare the lemon rind from the lemon and put into the water with the sugar.

2. Heat slowly until the sugar has dissolved then boil for 5 minutes.

3. Strain and set aside to cool.

4. Hull the strawberries reserving a few for decoration. Press the remainder through a nylon sieve and add the juice of half the lemon.

5. Whisk the egg whites until very stiff.

6. Combine all the ingredients well.

7. Put into an airtight container and place in the freezer.

8. Remove when half frozen, beat well and return to the freezer.

9. Place in the refrigerator about 1 hour before serving.

10. Serve in wine glasses topped with the whole berries.

TIME: Preparation takes 20 minutes, cooking takes 5 minutes.
Freezing takes about 8 hours.

COOK'S TIP: It is better to leave the sorbet in the freezer overnight at the end of Step 8.

LOW-FAT BROWN BREAD ICE CREAM

This ice-cream is ideal for slimmers.

SERVES 4

35g/1½ oz brown breadcrumbs
35g/1½ oz brown sugar
3 eggs, separated
280ml/½ pint Greek yogurt
1 dstsp honey (optional)

1. Place the breadcrumbs on a baking tray and cover with the sugar.

2. Place in a moderately hot oven 190°C/ 375°F/Gas Mark 5 for 20 minutes or until they begin to brown and caramelise. Stir once or twice so they brown evenly. Leave aside.

3. Beat the egg whites until stiff.

4. In a separate bowl, mix the egg yolks into the yogurt and then fold in the egg whites. Add the honey if desired and fold in evenly.

5. Add the cold breadcrumbs and mix well.

6. Place in the freezer and when setting point is reached stir the sides to prevent ice crystals forming.

7. Return to the freezer and leave until set.

TIME: Preparation takes 20 minutes, cooking and freezing takes 20 minutes plus 4-5 hours or overnight.

COOK'S TIP: Remove from the freezer and place in the refrigerator about ¾ of an hour before serving.

VARIATION: Maple syrup may be used in place of honey.

COFFEE AND RAISIN ICE CREAM

Perfect for a sweet finale or just as a treat

MAKES 20fl.oz/1 pint

280ml/½ pint full cream milk
100g/4oz sugar
6 tsps coffee granules or powder
1 tsp cocoa powder
1 egg yolk
1 tsp vanilla essence
280ml/½ pint whipping or double cream
50g/2oz raisins

1. Heat the milk and sugar until almost boiling.

2. Add the coffee and cocoa, stir and leave to cool.

3. Beat the egg yolk with the vanilla essence until frothy.

4. Whip the cream until stiff.

5. Pour the cream and coffee mixture into the egg mixture and stir well.

6. Add the raisins and stir again.

7. Freeze until firm (3-4 hours), stirring several times during freezing.

8. Defrost for 10-15 minutes before serving.

TIME: Preparation takes 3-4 hours, including freezing.

SERVING IDEA: Serve with home-made cookies.

VARIATION: For a chocolate flavour use light carob powder in place of coffee.

CASHEW ICE CREAM

For special occasions, just add 1 tbsp of rum for
an even more impressive ice-cream.

SERVES 4

1 large very ripe banana, peeled and
   roughly chopped
100g/4oz finely ground cashew nuts
140ml/¼ pint concentrated soya milk
½ tsp vanilla essence
2 tsps clear honey
2 rings unsweetened tinned pineapple,
   diced

1. Put all the ingredients, apart from the pineapple, into a blender and blend until smooth.

2. Add the pineapple and blend briefly.

3. Put the mixture in a shallow container and freeze for 2 hours.

TIME: Preparation takes 10 minutes, freezing takes 2 hours.

SERVING IDEA: Serve with strawberries or fresh fruit salad.

APRICOT FOOL

*Serve Apricot Fool in individual serving glasses, and
decorate with curls of carob chocolate.*

SERVES 4

225g/8oz dried apricots
1 ripe banana
1 small carton plain strained yogurt
1 egg
Few squares carob chocolate

1. Soak the apricots in water for at least 1 hour. Cook until soft then purée.

2. Mash the banana and add to the apricot purée.

3. Fold the yogurt into the fruit mixture.

4. Separate the egg and stir the yolk into fruit mixture.

5. Whisk the egg white until stiff then fold into the fruit mixture.

TIME: Preparation takes 10 minutes. Soaking and cooking takes about 2 hours 40 minutes.

VARIATION: Decorate with toasted almonds.

CRANBERRY FOOL

A simple and refreshing dessert.

SERVES 4

225g/8oz fresh cranberries
2 tbsps clear honey
75g/3oz whipping cream
100g/4oz Greek yogurt
Toasted almond flakes

1. Rinse the cranberries and stew with a scant amount of water until softened.

2. Remove from the heat, add the honey and leave to cool.

3. Whip the cream and gently fold in the yogurt.

4. Combine the yogurt and cream with the cooled cranberries.

5. Divide the mixture between four stem glasses and decorate with toasted almond flakes.

TIME: Preparation takes 10 minutes, cooking takes 15-20 minutes.

VARIATION: As fresh cranberries may be available only at Christmas time, redcurrants would make an excellent summer substitute.

LEMON TART

A classic dessert, loved by all age groups.

SERVES 6-8

100g/4oz vegetable fat
225g/8oz wholemeal flour
50g/2oz brown sugar
2 egg yolks
A little water

Filling
4 egg yolks
4 egg whites beaten
100g/4oz brown sugar
50g/2oz ground almonds
100g/4oz unsalted butter, softened
140ml/5fl.oz double cream, slightly
    whipped
2 lemons, rind and juice

1. Rub the fat into the flour until the mixture resembles fine breadcrumbs.

2. Mix in the sugar, add the egg yolks and a little water to mix.

3. Roll out to line a fairly deep flan tin.

4. Prick the bottom and bake blind in the oven for about 8 minutes at 210°C/425°F/Gas Mark 7.

5. Meanwhile, mix the egg yolks with the sugar and add the ground almonds, butter, whipped cream and lemon juice.

6. Beat until smooth and creamy and fold in the lemon rind and beaten egg white.

7. Pour into the pastry case and bake 180°C/350°F/Gas Mark 4 until slightly risen and golden brown.

8. Eat cold.

TIME: Preparation takes 25 minutes, cooking takes 48 minutes.

SERVING IDEA: Serve decorated with piped whipped cream.

WATCHPOINT: Do not overbeat the filling as it is liable to overflow during cooking.

ORANGE AND KIWI CHEESECAKE

Lemon could be used in place of orange if a tangy cheesecake is required.

SERVES 6-8

100g/4oz margarine
225g/8oz crushed wholemeal digestive
 biscuits

Topping
450g/1lb Quark or skimmed milk soft
 cheese
100g/4oz margarine
1 medium egg, beaten
Fruit and zest of 1 orange, chopped
25g/1oz ground almonds
¼ tsp almond essence
2 kiwi fruit

1. Make the base by melting the margarine and adding to the biscuit crumbs. Mix well and press into a dish or flan base.

2. Chill thoroughly.

3. Mix together the cheese, margarine, egg, chopped orange and zest, almonds, almond essence and one kiwi fruit, peeled and chopped.

4. Put onto base and smooth over the top.

5. Peel and slice the other kiwi-fruit and decorate the top of the cheesecake.

6. Chill for 2 hours.

TIME: Preparation takes 15 minutes. Chilling takes 2 hours.

SERVING IDEA: For a special occasion decorate with the kiwi fruit and halved and seeded black grapes.

PEACHY CHEESECAKE

A fairly rich cheesecake with a smooth texture.

SERVES 6

Base
12 digestive biscuits, crushed or liquidised
    until fine
40g/1½ oz melted butter or margarine

Topping
450g/14oz curd cheese
375ml/15fl.oz soured cream or Greek
    yogurt
2 tbsps clear honey
1½ tsps vanilla essence or lemon juice
2 eggs, beaten
1½ tbsps wholewheat self-raising flour
Sliced peaches to decorate

1. Preheat the oven to 150°C/300°F/Gas
Mark 2.

2. Combine the biscuit crumbs, melted
butter and spices and press the mixture in
the bottom of a greased 22.8cm/9" flan tin
or dish.

3. Combine the curd cheese and 200ml/
7fl.oz of the soured cream or yogurt, 1
tbsp honey, ¾ tsp vanilla essence, the
eggs and all the flour.

4. Pour the mixture onto the biscuit base
and bake in the preheated oven for
approximately 20 minutes or until just set.

5. Remove from the oven and increase the
oven temperature to 230°C/450°F/Gas
Mark 8.

6. Combine the remaining cream or yogurt
with the rest of the honey and vanilla
essence and spread over the top of the
cake. Smooth over with a knife or spatula.

7. Return to the oven and bake for 5
minutes.

8. Allow to cool before decorating with
sliced peaches.

9. Chill thoroughly before serving.

TIME: Preparation takes 25 minutes, cooking takes 25 minutes.

VARIATION: For special occasions decorate with seasonal fruit such as strawberries or
raspberries and carob curls.

COOK'S TIP: Sugar-free canned fruit may be used if fresh is not available.

CORN CAKE

This corn cake will freeze well.

MAKES 1 CAKE

675ml/23fl.oz milk
50g/2oz brown sugar
½ tsp vanilla essence
160g/5½ oz fine cornmeal
2 eggs
Pinch of salt
50g/2oz margarine

---

1. Line and grease a 17cm/7" loose bottomed cake tin.

2. Put the milk, sugar and vanilla essence into a saucepan and bring to the boil.

3. Stir in the cornmeal quickly to avoid forming lumps.

4. Remove the pan from the heat and allow to cool slightly.

5. Separate the eggs.

6. Beat the egg whites with a pinch of salt until it forms soft peaks.

7. Add the margarine and egg yolks, one at a time, to the cornmeal and beat well.

8. Stir in one spoonful of the egg white and then fold in the remainder carefully with a metal spoon.

9. Pour the mixture into a prepared tin and bake at 180°C/350°F/Gas Mark 4 for about 40 minutes.

10. Turn the cake onto a wire rack to cool.

TIME: Preparation takes 15 minutes, cooking takes 40 minutes.

SERVING IDEA: Decorate the top with fresh fruit and sprinkle nuts on the sides.

VARIATION: Use on a biscuit base to form a 'non-cheese cheesecake'.

CAROB APPLE CAKE

This cake is nicer if kept in an airtight tin for a day before serving.

MAKES 1 CAKE

150g/5oz soft margarine
100g/4oz light muscavado sugar
1 large egg, beaten
175g/6oz fine wholemeal flour
60g/2½ oz light carob powder
1½ tsps baking powder
1 tbsp Amontillado sherry
400g/14oz Bramley cooking apples,
   peeled and sliced

Topping
75g/3oz carob chips
Knob of butter
A little water

1. Cream the margarine and sugar together until fluffy.

2. Add half of the beaten egg and continue creaming.

3. Add the rest of the egg together with the sieved flour, carob and baking powder and sherry.

4. Place half of the mixture into a round 17.8cm/8" cake tin and cover with the sliced apples.

5. Add the other half of the mixture and smooth the top.

6. Bake at 160°C/325°F/Gas Mark 3 for 1¼ hours or until firm to the touch.

7. Melt the carob chips with the butter and water and drizzle over the top of the cake.

TIME: Preparation takes 25 minutes, cooking takes 1¼ hours.

SERVING IDEA: Serve hot with yogurt as a pudding or cold for afternoon tea.

DE-LUXE BREAD AND BUTTER PUDDING

Serve just as it is, hot from the oven.

SERVES 4

4 thin slices wholemeal bread
A little butter
Raspberry jam
2 eggs, beaten
450ml/¾ pint milk, warmed
2 tbsps single cream
3 tbsps light muscovado sugar
1 tsp vanilla essence
2 tbsps sultanas, soaked for 1 hour
1 tbsp dates
Grated nutmeg

1. Remove the crusts from the bread.

2. Sandwich the bread with the butter and jam and cut into small triangles.

3. Beat the eggs until fluffy.

4. Add the warmed milk, cream, sugar and vanilla.

5. Stir together well, making sure that the sugar has dissolved.

6. Arrange the bread triangles in a lightly buttered ovenproof dish so that they overlap and stand up slightly.

7. Scatter the dried fruits over the top.

8. Pour the egg, cream and milk mixture into the dish, ensuring that the bread triangles are saturated.

9. Grate a little nutmeg over the pudding and bake at 200°C/400°F/Gas Mark 6 for about 30 minutes.

TIME: Preparation takes 10 minutes, cooking takes 30 minutes.

VARIATION: Other flavoured jams may be used instead of raspberry jam.

CRANBERRY AND APPLE CRUMBLE

Serve hot with natural yogurt or serve cold with ice cream.

SERVES 4

675g/1½ lb Bramley or other cooking
  apples
50g/2oz raw cane sugar
175g/6oz fresh cranberries

Crumble
75g/3oz butter or margarine
50g/2oz sunflower seeds
75g/3oz raw cane or demerara sugar
150g/5oz wholewheat flour
50g/2oz Jumbo oats
50g/2oz porridge oats

1. Peel, core and dice the apples.

2. Place in a saucepan with the sugar and about 2 tbsps water.

3. Cook gently until just beginning to soften.

4. Add the cranberries and cook for a further minute. Remove from the heat.

5. Melt the butter or margarine in a small saucepan, add the sunflower seeds and fry very gently for a few minutes.

6. Meanwhile, mix together the other ingredients in a large bowl, rubbing in the raw cane sugar with the fingers if lumpy.

7. Pour the butter and sunflower seeds into this mixture and combine to form a loose crumble.

8. Place the fruit in a large, shallow oven-proof dish and sprinkle the crumble topping over.

9. Cook at 180°C/350°F/Gas Mark 4 for about 40 minutes or until the top is golden and crisp.

TIME: Preparation takes about 20 minutes, cooking takes 50 minutes.

RICE MERINGUE

*For convenience the rice pudding and apple purée can be
made in advance and assembled just before cooking the meringue.*

SERVES 4

25g/1oz short grain pudding rice
570ml/1 pint milk
Few drops almond essence
5 tbsps soft brown sugar
A little butter
2 large dessert apples
2 tbsps raspberry jam
2 egg whites

1. Wash the rice and put into a shallow, buttered ovenproof dish.

2. Add the milk, almond essence and 2 tbsps of soft brown sugar.

3. Dot with a little butter and bake for 2½-3 hours at 170°C/325°F/Gas Mark 3 stirring two or three times during cooking.

4. Remove from the oven.

5. Meanwhile, peel and core the apples. Slice finely and put into a saucepan with 1 tbsp of water.

6. Cook for 5-10 minutes until softened.

7. Add a little of the sugar to sweeten.

8. Cover the rice pudding with the raspberry jam.

9. Spread the apple purée over the top.

10. Grind the remaining sugar finely and beat the egg whites until they are very stiff.

11. Fold the sugar into the egg whites and cover the pudding with the meringue mixture.

12. With the back of a spoon, pull the meringue into 'peaks'.

13. Bake at 170°C/325°F/Gas Mark 3 for 20-30 minutes until heated through and golden on top.

14. Serve immediately.

TIME: Preparation takes 20 minutes, overall cooking takes about 3½ hours.

VARIATION: Make in individual ovenproof dishes.

Hot Apple Pizza

A delicious dessert – perfect with yogurt or cream.

SERVES 4-6

13g/½ oz fresh yeast
50ml/2fl.oz warm water, hand hot
75g/3oz strong wholemeal flour
50g/2oz strong white flour
½ tsp ground cinnamon
13g/½ oz butter or margarine
½ tbsp concentrated apple juice

Topping
2 red skinned dessert apples
25g/1oz raisins
25g/1oz hazelnuts
1 tbsp concentrated apple juice
13g/½ oz butter or margarine

1. Cream the yeast with the water, add 1 teaspoon of flour and leave in a warm place for 10-15 minutes until frothy.

2. Mix together the flours and cinnamon.

3. Rub in the butter.

4. Add the yeast mixture and concentrated apple juice to the flour.

5. Mix to a stiff dough, adding more warm water if necessary. Knead well.

6. Roll the dough into a circle, about 20.3/8" to 22.8/9" in diameter. Cover with cling film and leave to rise for 10-15 minutes.

7. Slice the apples evenly and arrange over the base.

8. Sprinkle the raisins, hazelnuts and concentratd apple juice over the apples and dot with the butter or margarine.

9. Bake on the middle shelf of the oven at 200°C/400°F/Gas Mark 6 for 15-20 minutes.

TIME: Preparation takes, including rising, 45 minutes. Cooking takes 15-20 minutes.

VARIATION: Use other fruits, except oranges in place of the apples.

PEAR AND APRICOT SLICE

Serve as a dessert or for afternoon tea topped with thick Greek yogurt.

MAKES 8 SLICES

2 pears, approximately 350g/12oz
100g/4oz dried apricots, soaked
1 tbsp clear honey
½ tbsp pear and apple spread
1 tbsp sunflower oil
1 egg
100g/4oz fine wholemeal flour
1 tsp baking powder
Flaked almonds to decorate

1. Peel and chop the pears into small pieces.

2. Chop the apricots finely.

3. Mix together the honey, pear and apple spread, and stir into the pears and apricots.

4. Add the oil and egg and mix well.

5. Mix together the flour and baking powder and fold into the pear and apricot mixture.

6. Spread the mixture in a greased 15cm x 20cm/6" x 8" tin.

7. Sprinkle with the flaked almonds.

8. Bake at 190°C/375°F/Gas Mark 5 for about 25 minutes or until risen and golden.

9. Leave to cool and cut into 8 fingers.

TIME: Preparation takes about 15 minutes, cooking takes 25 minutes.

COOK'S TIP: Pear and Apple Spread is sugar free and can be bought at most health food stores. It is an ideal substitute for jam.

BAKED RASPBERRY APPLES

A lovely combination which is perfectly complemented by cream or yogurt.

SERVES 6

2 tbsps concentrated apple juice
4 tbsps water
2 tbsps honey
1 tsp mixed spice
3 very large eating apples
225g/8oz raspberries

1. Put the concentrated apple juice, water, honey and mixed spice into a large bowl and mix together well.

2. Wash the apples and, with a sharp knife, make deep zig-zag cuts around each apple.

3. Take one half of the apple in each hand and twist gently until the two halves come apart.

4. Remove the core and immerse each apple in the apple juice mixture.

5. Place the apples in an ovenproof dish and bake at 200°C/400°F/Gas Mark 6 for 20-25 minutes until just soft.

6. Remove from the oven and top with the raspberries.

7. Pour the remaining apple juice mixture over the raspberries and return to the oven, 150°C/300°F/Gas Mark 2 for 10 minutes.

8. Serve at once.

TIME: Preparation takes 10 minutes, cooking takes 30-35 minutes.

SERVING IDEA: Serve topped with a spoonful of Greek yogurt or whipped cream.

COOK'S TIP: Frozen raspberries may be used but make sure they are well thawed out.

CAROB PEARS

Children in particular will love these tasty pears.

SERVES 4

---

4 ripe dessert pears
1 tbsp maple syrup
Boiling water to cover
50g/2oz carob bar
25g/1oz dessicated coconut

---

1. Peel the pears thinly, leaving the stalk intact.

2. Cut a small slice from the base of each pear so they will stand upright and place in a bowl.

3. Mix the maple syrup with the boiling water and pour over the pears. Leave to go cold.

4. Remove the pears from the syrup and dry carefully. Place in one large or four small serving dishes.

5. Break up the carob bar and put it into a heatproof bowl.

6. Stand the bowl in a saucepan of boiling water until melted, stirring from time to time.

7. Spoon the melted carob over the pears, allow to set a little before sprinkling the dessicated coconut over the top.

8. Refrigerate for 2-3 hours.

TIME: Preparation takes 10 minutes, cooling takes 30 minutes.

SERVING IDEA: Serve with piped whipped cream or yogurt.

FRUIT SALAD TRIFLE

*As this recipe makes two halves of sponge and only
one is needed for the trifle, the other half
can be frozen for use on a subsequent occasion.*

SERVES 6

Carob Sponge
100g/4oz soft margarine
75g/3oz light muscovado sugar, finely
    ground
2 eggs (size 3)
75g/3oz wholemeal flour, sieved
25g/1oz carob powder
1½ tsps baking powder

Trifle
6 tbsps apple juice
Apricot or banana liquer (optional)
2 crisps eating apples, cored and chopped
    but not skinned
1 large banana, sliced
2 oranges, peeled, segmented and roughly
    chopped
Half a pineapple, diced
50g/2oz dates, chopped
50g/2oz hazelnuts
100g/4oz whipping cream
100g/4oz Greek yogurt
Few grapes, halved and de-seeded

1. Cream the margarine and sugar together
until pale and fluffy.

2. Add the eggs, one at a time, then
carefully fold in the sieved flour, carob
powder and baking powder.

3. Turn into two greased 17.8cm/7"
sponge or flan tins and bake for 20
minutes at 180°C/350°F/Gas Mark 4 until
golden brown and risen.

4. Leave to cool.

5. Place one of the carob sponges into a
trifle bowl and saturate with the apple
juice. Leave for half an hour.

6. Add the liquer, fruits and nuts, making
sure they are equally distributed through
the bowl.

7. Whip the cream until stiff and fold in
the yogurt.

8. Spread over the trifle.

9. With the back of a fork, trace from the
rim of the bowl into the centre, making a
lined effect.

10. Chill before serving.

TIME: Preparation takes 30 minutes, cooking takes 30 minutes.

SERVING IDEA: Serve decorated with orange segments, pineapple cubes and carob chips.

CARIBBEAN PINEAPPLE

An impressive and delicious dessert which is easy to prepare.

SERVES 6-8

1 large fresh pineapple
150ml/5fl.oz double cream
1 quantity of Coffee and Raisin Ice-Cream
  (see index)
125ml/4fl.oz rum
2 tbsps chopped mixed nuts

1. Slice the top off the pineapple at the shoulder and scoop out the flesh from the top.

2. Using a sharp knife, cut just within the skin around the circumference until the bottom is almost reached.

3. Insert the blade 2.5cm/1" up from the base and cut round in both directions just enough to loosen the flesh. Do not cut the bottom off.

4. Insert a fork into the top of the pineapple flesh and twist to remove. Drain the cask and place in the freezer.

5. Remove the hard core from the pineapple and chop the flesh into tiny pieces, drain well.

6. Whip the cream until stiff.

7. In a large bowl, break up the ice-cream with a wooden spoon.

8. Add the cream and nuts and mix well.

9. Sprinkle this mixture with half of the rum.

10. Fill the frozen pineapple cask with the mixture, replace the top and wrap carefully in foil.

11. Return to the deep freeze until required. Any extra mixture can be frozen in a small bowl.

12. To serve, transfer the pineapple to the refrigerator three quarter of an hour before required.

13. Place a serving dish in the oven to become very hot.

14. Put the pineapple on hot dish, pour the rest of the rum onto the dish and a little on the sides of the cask and light it.

15. Scoop out a portion of the ice-cream into individual serving dishes and spoon over a little burnt rum.

TIME: Preparation takes 20 minutes.

VARIATION: Use plain vanilla ice-cream and add 1 tablespoonful of instant coffee powder and 50g/2oz of raisins to the whipped cream.

BANANA FLAVOURED APRICOTS WITH COCONUT CREAM

Make this dessert a day ahead and serve straight from the fridge.

SERVES 4

175g/6oz dried apricots
280ml/½ pint banana flavoured soya milk
   plus 3 extra tbsps
140ml/¼ pint water
100g/4oz creamed coconut, grated
Juice of ½ lemon

1. Chop the apricots finely and put into a bowl.

2. Pour the ½ pint soya milk over the top.

3. Heat the water in a pan and stir in the creamed coconut until it has dissolved. Allow to cool a little.

4. Put the creamed coconut, lemon juice and 3 tbsps soya milk into a blender and blend until smooth.

5. Cover the apricots and cream with cling film and refrigerate overnight.

TIME: Preparation takes 10 minutes, cooking takes 2 minutes. Refrigerate overnight.

SERVING IDEA: Serve in individual serving dishes topped with spoonfuls of the coconut cream.

VARIATION: Plain soya milk may be used if banana flavoured soya milk is not available.

MINTED GRAPES

A refreshing dessert to serve after a large meal.

SERVES 4

275g/10oz green grapes
A little Creme de Menthe
125ml/4fl.oz soured cream
Soft brown sugar

1. Halve and de-seed the grapes.

2. Divide the grapes equally between four serving glasses.

3. Sprinkle with a little Creme de Menthe.

4. Top with soured cream.

5. Sprinkle a little brown sugar over and serve at once.

TIME: Preparation takes 10 minutes.

SERVING IDEA: Serve garnished with mint leaves.

VARIATION: Use sherry in place of the Creme de Menthe and yogurt instead of soured cream.

GINGER LOG

Omit the sherry from this dish and it becomes the perfect kid's treat.

SERVES 6

1 x 200g/7oz packet ginger biscuits
2fl.oz sherry
280ml/½ pint double cream
225g/8oz tin pineapple chunks
Chopped nuts, toasted

1. Unwrap the ginger biscuits and set aside any broken ones.

2. Pour a little sherry into a small bowl.

3. Whip the cream until thick and divide into two.

4. Drain the pineapple chunks, divide into two and chop one half very finely.

5. Mix into half of the cream.

6. Briefly, dip each biscuit into the sherry and, using the cream and pineapple mixture, sandwich the ginger biscuits together to make a log.

7. Lay the log on a serving dish and cover with the other half of the whipped cream spreading evenly with a knife.

8. Using a fork, 'lift' the cream into peaks.

9. Refrigerate for at least 2 hours.

10. Sprinkle with chopped nuts and decorate with the remaining pineapple chunks.

TIME: Preparation takes 10 minutes. Refrigeration takes 2 hours.

SERVING IDEA: Cut diagonally to serve.

VARIATION: Sprinkle with toasted coconut instead of nuts.

STRAWBERRY CLOUD

It takes no time at all to make this delightful summer dessert.

SERVES 4-6

450g/1lb strawberries
1 x 275g/10oz pack silken tofu
Juice of ½ lemon
2 tbsps soft brown sugar
Few drops vanilla essence

1. Wash and hull the strawberries. Leave a few on one side to decorate.

2. Drain the tofu and put into the liquidiser together with the strawberries, lemon juice and sugar.

3. Liquidise until smooth.

4. Add vanilla essence to taste and mix well.

5. Divide the mixture between 4-6 individual serving dishes and decorate with the reserved strawberries.

6. Chill until required.

TIME: Preparation takes 5-8 minutes.

SERVING IDEA: For a special occasion, pipe whipped cream around the edges of the serving dishes.

VARIATION: Other fruits such as apples or peaches may be used instead but they will not produce such a colourful dessert.

CHERRY BERRY MEDLEY

A pretty combination, perfect for summer lunches.

SERVES 6

450ml/¾ pint water
100g/4oz soft brown sugar
1 tsp mixed spice
225g/8oz redcurrants
450g/1lb strawberries
225g/8oz raspberries
225g/8oz cherries, stoned

1. Put the water, sugar and spice into a pan.

2. Boil for 5 minutes.

3. Put the redcurrants into a heatproof bowl and pour over the boiling liquid.

4. Leave to cool.

5. When cold, add the strawberries, raspberries and cherries.

6. Stir well and refrigerate for at least 2 hours before serving.

TIME: Preparation takes 10 minutes, cooking takes 5 minutes. Cooling and refrigeration takes 2 hours 15 minutes.

SERVING IDEA: Serve with ice-cream and French wafer biscuits.

VARIATION: If using blackberries in place of raspberries, treat in the same way as the redcurrants.

KOMPOT (DRIED FRUIT SALAD)

*This classic Middle Eastern dish is simple
to prepare and can be made well in advance.*

SERVES 6-8

225g/8oz dried prunes
225g/8oz dried apricots
100g/4oz dried figs
100g/4oz raisins
100g/4oz blanched almonds
50g/2oz pine kernels
1 tsp cinnamon
¼ tsp nutmeg
100g/4oz brown sugar
1 tbsp culinary rose water
Juice and zest of 1 orange

1. Stone the prunes and chop roughly.

2. Halve the apricots and quarter the figs.

3. Place them in a large bowl and add the rest of the ingredients.

4. Cover with cold water.

5. Stir well and keep in a cool place for 1-2 days, stirring a couple of times each day.

6. Before serving, mix again well.

TIME: Preparation takes 15 minutes. Standing time 1-2 days.

SERVING IDEA: Place the mixture in a glass serving dish, and serve with yogurt or cream.

COOK'S TIP: After 24 hours the liquid in which the Kompot is soaking will become very thick and syrupy. If you need to add more liquid, add a little orange juice.

VARIATION: Other dried fruits may be used but keep to the same quantities. Pistachio nuts can take the place of blanched almonds.

BAKING

There is something very satisfying about producing batches of home-made bread, biscuits and cakes even if they get eaten before they have time to cool down!

Wholefood cookery means using wholemeal, wholewheat and wheatmeal flours. 100 per cent wholewheat or wholemeal flours are suitable for making breads, pastry and heavier cakes, whereas 80-90 per cent flours have a finer texture and are suitable for pastries, sponges, scones and biscuits.

Most recipes using white flour can be easily adapted by replacing all or some of it with brown flour. To begin with it may be best trying half white flour and half brown as this will give an idea of the different tastes and textures you can achieve by altering the flours. If you like this mix then continue to use it or adapt the ratio of white to brown to suit your taste.

Fats are important in baking and the only restriction for vegetarians are lard and suet, both of which are obtained from animals. Vegetarian suet is readily available and lard is easily replaced with vegetable fats. Here vegetarians have a health advantage, as most fats and oils of vegetable origin are unsaturated, whereas those derived from animals are of the more unhealthy, saturated, nature.

MRS. MURPHY'S WHOLEWHEAT BROWN BREAD

This is a very moist bread which will last for days.

MAKES 2 LOAVES

750g/1½ lbs wholewheat flour
1 cup white flour
1 cup porridge oats
1 cup bran
1 cup pinhead oatmeal
½ cup wheatgerm
½ tsp baking soda
½ tsp sea salt
1.2 ltrs/2 pints milk
2 eggs, beaten

1. Heat the oven to 180°C/350°F/ Gas Mark 4.

2. Mix all the dry ingredients together.

3. Mix the eggs and milk and add to the dry ingredients.

4. Spoon into 2 greased 1lb loaf tins and bake in the centre of the oven for 1¼ to 1½ hours.

5. Turn out to cool on a wire rack.

TIME: Preparation takes about 20 minutes, cooking takes 1¼ to 1½ hours.

VARIATION: A handful of caraway seeds can be added to the mixture and some sprinkled on the top before baking.

QUICK HOME-MADE BREAD

*The molasses in this recipe gives the
bread an attractive appearance.*

MAKES 3 LOAVES

1150ml/2 pints hand hot water
1 tbsp molasses
1 tbsp sunflower oil
1.5kg/3.3lbs 100% wholemeal flour
2 sachets 'Allison's Easy-Bake Yeast'
3 tsps sea salt

---

1. Set the oven to 220°C/425°F/
Gas Mark 7.

2. Oil three 900g/2lbs bread tins and place
them on top of a warm cooker.

3. Fill two 570ml/1 pint jugs with the hand
hot water.

4. Add the molasses and oil to one of the
jugs, mix and set aside.

5. Place the flour, yeast and salt into a
large bowl and mix together thoroughly.

6. Gradually pour the water and molasses
mixture into the flour, mixing in with your
hands.

7. Add the other jug of water bit by bit
until the dough is wettish but not sticky.
You may have some water left over.

8. Knead the dough about a dozen times.

9. Divide the dough between the three
tins and press down firmly.

10. Leave to rise on the top of the cooker
for 5-10 minutes or until the dough has
risen near to the top of the tins.

11. Bake in the preheated oven for 35-40
minutes.

TIME: Preparation takes 20 minutes, cooking takes 35-40 minutes.

FREEZING: This bread will freeze well.

RICH STOLLEN BREAD

*This makes an attractive centre-piece on the tea table,
particularly around Christmas time.*

MAKES 1 LOAF

250g/9oz strong unbleached white flour
Pinch of salt
12g/½ oz fresh yeast
12g/½ oz light muscovado sugar
87ml/3½ fl.oz milk, warmed
1 egg, beaten

Filling
1 egg
150g/5oz ground almonds
50g/2oz poppy seeds, plus extra for
    decoration
50g/2oz raisins, soaked overnight
50g/2oz currants
50g/2oz cherries, chopped
50g/2oz light muscovado sugar, finely
    ground
25g/1oz dates, chopped
Juice of half a lemon
Almond essence

50g/2oz margarine
1 egg, beaten to glaze

1. Place the flour and salt in a bowl.

2. Cream the yeast and sugar together,
add the milk and stir well.

3. Add the beaten egg and leave for a few
minutes in a warm place.

4. Add the mixture to the flour and mix.
Knead well for 5 minutes.

5. Put into a clean bowl, cover and leave
to prove in a warm place for 40 minutes.

6. To make the filling, beat the egg,
reserving a little, and add all the other
filling ingredients. Mix well – the mixture
should be fairly moist.

7. To assemble, knock back the dough
and roll out to a rectangle 30.5cm x
20.3cm/12" x 8".

8. Dot 25g/1oz of the margarine over two
thirds of the dough from the top. Fold
over from the bottom to one third up,
then fold from top to bottom. Seal edges
and make one quarter turn.

9. Roll out to a rectangle shape again and
repeat with the remainder of the
margarine. Fold over as before but do not
roll out.

10. Place in the refrigerator for about half
an hour. Remove and roll out a rectangle
as before.

11. Cover with the filling, leaving a tiny
margin around the edges. Roll up width-
ways to make a fat sausage shape and
tuck in the ends. Brush with beaten egg.

12. Mark out in 2.5cm/1" slices, snipping
either side with scissors.

13. Cover with the remaining almond
flakes and poppy seeds and leave to
prove for a further 15 minutes.

14. Bake at 200°C/400°F/Gas Mark 6 for
30 minutes.

TIME: Preparation takes 25 minutes, cooking takes 30 minutes.
Proving takes 1 hour 40 minutes.

SOFT BREAD CAKES

The bread cakes may be split and toasted, buttered and then filled with sizzling cheese or fried eggs to make a nutritious and satisfying snack meal.

MAKES 6

350g/12oz wholewheat flour
1 tsp salt
25g/1oz fresh yeast
1 tsp brown sugar
1 tea cup of milk
25g/1oz vegetable fat
1 egg, beaten

1. Put the flour and salt in a mixing bowl.

2. Cream the yeast and sugar together until liquid.

3. Warm the milk with the vegetable fat.

4. Mix the milk and fat with the creamed yeast and stir in the beaten egg.

5. Make a hollow in the flour and work the milk mixture in gradually to make a soft dough.

6. Knead a little and form into six round cakes.

7. Cover and leave to rise for 20 minutes in a warm place.

8. Bake 220°C/425°F/Gas Mark 7 for about 15 minutes.

9. Glaze with beaten egg or milk and sugar a few minutes before removing from the oven.

TIME: Preparation takes 30 minutes, cooking takes 15 minutes.

VARIATION: Make Currant Tea Cakes by adding 75g/3oz currants and 50g/2oz sugar to the recipe in the mixing.

GRANARY ROLLS

*For a crisp crust brush the rolls with salted water
and sprinkle with cracked wheat before baking.*

MAKES 10

12oz granary flour
1 tsp salt
25g/1oz vegetable fat
12g/½ oz fresh yeast or 2 tsps dried yeast
1 tsp brown sugar
225ml/8fl.oz warm water

1. Place the granary flour and salt in a mixing bowl and leave in a warm place.

2. Melt the vegetable fat in a pan and leave to cool.

3. Cream the yeast and sugar together with three-quarters of the warm water.

4. Make a well in the middle of the flour and pour in the yeast mixture.

5. Add the melted fat and mix to a pliable dough, adding the remaining water as necessary.

6. Knead lightly for a minute or two.

7. Cover with a clean tea towel and leave in a warm place until the dough has doubled in size.

8. Knead again for 3-5 minutes and shape into 10 smooth rolls.

9. Place well apart on a floured baking tray, cover and leave in a warm place until the rolls have doubled in size.

10. Bake in the centre of a preheated oven, 220°C/425°F/Gas Mark 7 for 15-20 minutes or until the rolls sound hollow when tapped underneath.

11. Cool on a wire rack.

TIME: Preparation and proving takes 1 hour, cooking takes 15-20 minutes.

FREEZING: The rolls will freeze well for up to 1 month. Allow to thaw for 1 hour at room temperature before use.

SCOFA BREAD

*The ideal chunky bread to serve warm with
a ploughman's lunch or lunchtime salad meals.*

MAKES 1 LOAF

550g/1¼lbs self-raising wholemeal flour
225g/8oz bran
1 tsp salt
100g/4oz vegetable fat
Just under 570ml/1 pint water
1 tbsp vegetable oil

1. Put the flour, bran and salt into a mixing bowl.

2. Rub in the fat and mix the water and oil together.

3. Make a well in the centre of the flour and pour in the water and oil.

4. Mix in the flour, drawing it into the liquid mixture gradually from the sides, until a dough is formed.

5. Shape into a 17.8cm/7" round and place on a greased baking tray.

6. With a sharp knife cut to within 1.2cm/½" of the bottom making four sections.

7. Bake just above the centre of the oven, 200°C/400°F/Gas Mark 6 for about 1 hour or until nicely browned and 'hollow' sounding when tapped with the back of your fingers.

8. Remove from the oven and wrap in a clean tea towel to cool.

TIME: Preparation takes 10 minutes, cooking takes 1 hour.

COOK'S TIP: Eat within a couple of days.

YOGURT SCONES

Serve with jam and cream.

MAKES 10 SCONES

50g/2oz vegetable margarine or butter
200g/8oz wholemeal self-raising flour
25g/1oz demerara sugar
50g/1oz raisins
Plain yogurt to mix

1. Rub the fat into the flour and sugar.

2. Add the raisins and mix well.

3. Add enough yogurt to mix to a fairly stiff dough.

4. Turn the mixture out onto a floured board and knead lightly. Make two large circles of dough or cut into 2" rounds.

5. Bake in hot oven for 15-17 minutes at 210°C/425°F/Gas Mark 7.

6. Remove and cool on a wire rack.

TIME: Preparation takes 10 minutes, cooking takes 15-17 minutes.

VARIATION: Use chopped dried apricots instead of raisins.

SUCCULENT SCONES

These scones make an ideal accompaniment
for soup in place of bread.

MAKES 6-8 SCONES

225g/8oz wholemeal flour
225g/8oz unbleached white flour
1 scant tsp salt
1 scant tsp bicarbonate of soda
1 scant tsp cream of tartar
50g/2oz unsalted butter
1 egg, well beaten
140ml/¼ pint natural yogurt
Milk

1. Preheat the oven to 220°C/425°F/Gas Mark 7.

2. Sift the flours, salt, soda and cream of tartar twice and put into a mixing bowl.

3. Rub in the butter.

4. Put the yogurt into a measuring jug and make up to 280ml/½ pint with milk, stir well.

5. Quickly stir the beaten egg into the flour followed by the yogurt and milk.

6. When the mixture has formed a soft dough, knead for a few seconds.

7. Divide the dough into 6 or 8 pieces and form into approximate rounds on an oiled baking sheet.

8. Flatten the dough with your fingers.

9. Prick with a fork.

10. Bake for 8-10 minutes or until just coloured.

TIME: Preparation takes about 15 minutes, cooking takes 8-10 minutes.

VARIATION: Add 2oz of presoaked raisins or sultanas and serve for afternoon tea.

OATLET COOKIES

A delicious mix of oats, seeds and syrup
makes these cookies extra special.

MAKES 10 COOKIES

100g/4oz porridge oats
100g/4oz plain flour
85g/3oz sunflower seeds
25g/1oz sesame seeds
½ tsp mixed spice
100g/4oz margarine
1 tbsp brown sugar
1 tsp golden syrup or molasses
½ tsp bread soda
1 tbsp boiling water
200g/8oz carob drops

1. Mix the oats, flour, sunflower seeds, sesame seeds and spice together.

2. Melt the margarine, sugar and golden syrup or molasses over a gentle heat.

3. Add the bread soda and water to the syrup mixture and stir well.

4. Pour over dry ingredients and mix.

5. Place spoonfuls of the mixture well apart onto a greased baking tray and bake for 10 minutes at 190°C/375°F/Gas Mark 5.

6. Allow to cool on the tray.

7. Melt the carob drops in a bowl over hot water and place teaspoonsful of the melted carob on top of the cookies. Leave to set. Store in an airtight tin.

TIME: Preparation takes 15 minutes, cooking takes 10 minutes.

VARIATION: Ground ginger can be used in place of the mixed spice.

COOK'S TIP: A block of carob may be used in place of the carob drops.

SUSAN'S OATIES

*For a super taste add finely chopped nuts or
desiccated coconut to this recipe.*

MAKES ABOUT 20 BISCUITS

100g/4oz margarine
100g/4oz brown sugar
1 tsp molasses
1 tsp boiling water
1 tsp bicarbonate of soda
100g/4oz wholemeal flour
100g/4oz oats
½ tsp baking powder

1. Melt the margarine, sugar and molasses
in a saucepan.

2. Add the boiling water and bicarbonate
of soda.

3. Remove from the heat and stir in the
flour, oats and baking powder.

4. Place teaspoons of the mixture onto
greased baking sheets.

5. Bake at 160°C/325°F/Gas Mark 3 for 20
minutes.

6. Remove from the baking sheets and
place on a wire tray to cool.

TIME: Preparation takes 10 minutes, cooking takes 20 minutes.

COOK'S TIP: Use 50g/2oz oats and 50g/2oz desiccated coconut,
but reduce the amount of sugar.

AMARETTI-ALMOND MACAROONS

Serve these delicious macaroons with tea or coffee.

MAKES ABOUT 24

225g/8oz whole almonds
225g/8oz unrefined granulated sugar
2 egg whites
1 tsp almond essence

1. Blanch the almonds by plunging them into boiling water for 2 minutes.

2. Skin the almonds and spread them over a baking sheet.

3. Dry off in a warm oven for a few minutes without browning.

4. Grind the granulated sugar until it resembles fine caster sugar.

5. Grind the almonds.

6. Sieve the sugar and almonds together.

7. In a large bowl, beat the egg whites until stiff but not dry.

8. Gradually fold in the almond and sugar mixture and add the almond essence.

9. Pipe or spoon the mixture onto a floured baking sheet, alternatively put the mixture on to sheets of rice paper.

10. Leave for as long as possible to rest before baking.

11. Preheat the oven to 180°C/350°F/Gas Mark 4.

12. Bake for 15-20 minutes until golden brown.

13. Transfer the cooked macaroons to a cooling rack.

TIME: Preparation takes 15 minutes, cooking takes 15-20 minutes.

COOK'S TIP: The macaroons should be crisp on the outside but have a rather chewy centre. Longer cooking will crisp them all the way through if desired.

SHORTBREAD BISCUITS

*Sandwich these biscuits together with raspberry
jam for children's birthday parties.*

MAKES ABOUT 18

150g/5oz unbleached white flour
37g/2½ oz light muscovado sugar, finely
    ground
100g/4oz soft margarine
½ tsp vanilla essence

1. Sieve the flour and sugar together and rub in the margarine.

2. Add the vanilla essence and bind the mixture together.

3. Form into small balls and place on a baking tray a few inches apart.

4. With the back of a fork, press the balls down making a criss-cross pattern.

5. Bake at 190°/375°F/Gas Mark 4 for about 10-15 minutes until golden brown in colour.

6. Cool and store in an airtight container.

TIME: Preparation takes 10 minutes, cooking takes 10-15 minutes.

VARIATIONS: Add a tablespoon of currants to make fruit biscuits.
Omit the vanilla essence and substitute almond essence to make almond biscuits.

GINGER SNAPS

A great favourite for tea breaks.

MAKES 18-20

100g/4oz plain wholemeal flour
1½ level tsps baking powder
1½ level tsps ground ginger
50g/2oz soft brown sugar
Rind and juice of ½ lemon
3 tbsps golden syrup
50g/2oz margarine

1. Sift the flour, baking powder, ginger and sugar into a mixing bowl.

2. Add the lemon rind and juice.

3. Melt the syrup and margarine over a low heat and stir into the dry ingredients.

4. Leave to cool.

5. Roll into small balls and place well apart on greased baking trays.

6. Flatten out slightly with the back of a fork, still keeping their shape.

7. Cook at 190°C/375°F/Gas Mark 5 for 10-15 minutes.

8. Allow to cool for 2 minutes and then remove to a wire rack.

TIME: Preparation takes 10 minutes, cooking takes 10-15 minutes.

VARIATION: Substitute cinnamon for the ginger and sprinkle with chopped nuts.

COOK'S TIP: As the biscuits cool they will become crisp. Store in an airtight tin.

CRUNCH

If kept for a couple of days the Crunch will become deliciously soft and sticky.

MAKES 24 SQUARES

225g/8oz butter or margarine
2 tbsps golden syrup
5 cups oats
1 cup soft brown sugar

1. Put the butter and syrup into a pan and melt gently over a low heat.

2. Place the oats into a large mixing bowl and mix in the sugar.

3. Pour the melted butter and syrup over the oats and mix well with a wooden spoon.

4. Put the mixture into a 30.5cm x 20.3cm/ 12" x 8" Swiss roll tin and flatten well with the back of a spoon.

5. Bake in the centre of a 180°C/350°F/ Gas Mark 4 oven for 30-35 minutes until golden brown on top.

6. Remove from the oven, allow to cool for 2-3 minutes and mark into squares.

7. Leave until nearly cold before removing.

8. Store in an airtight tin.

TIME: Preparation takes 10 minutes, cooking takes 30-35 minutes.

VARIATION: Use 3 cups of oats and 2 cups of unsweetened muesli.

CHOC-OAT SLICES

Perfect for the lunch box or a kiddies party.

MAKES 12 SLICES

100g/4oz carob bar
100g/4oz hard margarine
1 tbsp clear honey
225g/8oz porridge oats
100g/4oz sultanas
50g/2oz dessicated coconut

1. Break the carob into a pan and add the margarine and honey.

2. Melt over a very low heat and stir until all the ingredients have melted.

3. Remove from the heat and add the oats, sultanas and coconut.

4. Spread the mixture evenly into a greased rectangular baking tin and bake at 180°C/350°F/Gas Mark 4 for 25-30 minutes.

5. Cool slightly and cut into slices.

6. When completely cold, remove and store in an airtight tin.

TIME: Preparation takes 10 minutes, cooking takes 25-30 minutes.

VARIATION: Raisins may be used in place of the sultanas.
Try maple syrup instead of honey.

CAROB BISCUIT CAKE

A very rich and delicious cake.

MAKES 16 SQUARES

225g/8oz digestive biscuits
100g/4oz margarine or butter
1 tbsp brown sugar
3 level tbsps carob powder
2 tbsps golden syrup
1 cup sultanas
225g/8oz carob bar

1. Crush the biscuits with a rolling pin and place in a mixing bowl.

2. Put the margarine, sugar, carob powder and syrup into a pan and melt over a low heat, stirring all the time.

3. Add to the biscuit crumbs together with the sultanas.

4. Mix very thoroughly.

5. Press the mixture into a 20.3cm/8" square container.

6. Break the carob bar into a heatproof bowl and place over a pan of simmering water until melted.

7. Cover the cake with the melted carob and mark it with the back of a fork.

8. Refrigerate until cold.

9. Cut into squares and store in an airtight tin.

TIME: Preparation takes 20-25 minutes plus chilling time.

CARROT CAKE WITH APRICOT FILLING

This cake will freeze well for up to 2 months.

MAKES 1 CAKE

100g/4oz dried apricots
175g/6oz butter or margarine
175g/6oz brown sugar
2 eggs, separated
200g/7oz plain flour
1 tsp baking powder
225g/8oz carrots (150g/5oz weight when peeled and finely grated)
50g/2oz sultanas
75g/3oz walnuts, finely chopped
2 tsps grated lemon rind
½ tsp ground cinnamon

1. Soak the apricots in water overnight, drain and purée until smooth.

2. Grease a 17.8cm/7" round spring mould tin or cake tin.

3. Beat the butter and sugar together until pale and creamy.

4. Whisk the egg yolks and beat into the butter and sugar.

5. Sieve the flour and baking powder and fold into the mixture.

6. Add the rest of the ingredients except the egg whites.

7. Whisk the egg whites until they form soft peaks, and fold into the mixture.

8. Place the mixture in the greased tin and cook at 180°C/350°F/Gas Mark 4 for 45-50 minutes.

9. Cool in the tin for 10 minutes and then turn out onto a wire rack.

10. When completely cooled, slice in half and spoon the puréed apricot mixture onto the bottom half. Place the other half on top.

TIME: Preparation takes 20 minutes, cooking takes 45-50 minutes.

VARIATION: Replace the apricots with dried pears.

VIENNA CAKE

A versatile cake which can be adapted to suit any occasion.

SERVES 8-10

225g/8oz butter or margarine
225g/8oz Barbados sugar
3 eggs, separated
3 tbsps milk
75g/3oz carob powder
225g/8oz wholemeal flour
175g/6oz carob bar

1. Place the butter and sugar in a mixing bowl and cream together.

2. Add the egg yolks and beat well.

3. Mix in the milk.

4. Combine the carob powder with the flour and fold into the creamed mixture, which will be very stiff at this point.

5. Beat the egg whites until they are stiff and fold gently into the mixture.

6. Put everything into a lined 17.8cm/7" cake tin and bake at 150°C/300°F/Gas mark 2 for 1½ hours until a skewer inserted into the centre comes out clean.

7. Turn out onto a wire rack to cool.

8. When the cake is completely cold, melt the carob bar in a bowl over a pan of simmering water.

9. Cover the cake with the melted carob, smoothing it with a knife dipped in boiling water.

10. Leave to harden before storing in an airtight tin.

TIME: Preparation takes 20 minutes, cooking takes 1½ hours.

SERVING IDEA: Serve with thickly whipped cream.

VARIATION: Instead of covering with carob, make into a gateau by filling with cream and topping with fruits. For a rich tea-time cake add 100g/4oz of chopped walnuts to the basic mixture.

RICH FRUIT CAKE WITH GUINNESS

A deliciously moist fruit cake which is easy to make.

MAKES 1 CAKE

225g/8oz soft margarine
225g/8oz dark brown sugar
4 medium eggs
275g/10oz wholemeal flour
1 dstsp mixed spice
500g/1lb 2oz mixed dried fruit
10 tbsps Guinness

1. Cream the margarine and sugar together.

2. Beat in the eggs one at a time.

3. Gradually stir in the flour and mixed spice.

4. Mix in the dried fruit.

5. Add 4 tbsps Guinness to mix.

6. Place the mixture into a 17.8cm/7" loose-bottomed cake tin and make a deep well in the centre, this allows the finished cake to have a flat top.

7. Cook for 1 hour at 170°C/325°F/Gas Mark 3 and then turn down to 150°C/300°F/Gas Mark 2 for a further 1½ hours.

8. Allow the cake to cool in the tin.

9. Remove and turn upside down. Prick the base of the cake all over with a skewer and slowly pour over the remaining 6 tbsps of Guinness.

10. Store in a cool place for at least a week before eating.

TIME: Preparation takes about 15 minutes, cooking takes 2½ hours.

SERVING IDEA: Use for birthdays and special occasions or serve with chunks of tasty cheese.

VARIATION: This mixture can be cooked in two 1lb loaf tins, reduce the final cooking time and cook until a skewer inserted into the cake comes out clean.

BANANA LOAF

Eat on its own as a cake or slice thinly and
butter to serve for elevenses or afternoon tea.

MAKES 1 LOAF

1 tea cup of porridge oats
1 tea cup of sugar
1 tea cup of mixed fruit
1 tea cup of Granose banana soya milk
1 breakfast cup of self-raising flour
Pinch of nutmeg

1. Begin preparing the cake the day before it is to be cooked. Place all the ingredients except the self-raising flour and nutmeg into a large bowl and stir well.

2. Cover and put into the refrigerator overnight.

3. The following day, line or grease a 1lb loaf tin.

4. Mix the self-raising flour and the nutmeg gently into the mixture and put into the loaf tin.

5. Bake at 180°C/350°F/Gas Mark 4 for an hour or until a skewer inserted into the loaf comes out clean.

TIME: Preparation takes 10 minutes, cooking takes 1 hour.

VARIATIONS: ½ a tsp of mixed spice may be used in place of the nutmeg. Ordinary milk or plain soya milk can be used instead of banana soya milk.

SERVING IDEA: Eat on its own as a cake or slice thinly and butter to serve for elevenses or afternoon tea.

COOK'S TIP: The loaf becomes more moist if left in an airtight tin for a day or two before eating.

PRUNE AND WALNUT LOAF

If you do not have prunes, dates taste just as good.

MAKES 1 LOAF

350g/12oz prunes
175ml/6fl.oz water
350g/12oz fine wholemeal flour
2 tsps baking powder
50g/2oz brown sugar
1 tsp mixed spice
100g/4oz walnuts, chopped
4 tbsps sunflower oil
1 egg
Orange juice
Whole walnuts to decorate

1. Simmer the prunes in the water until soft.

2. Allow to cool, retain the cooking liquid, remove the stones and chop finely.

3. Mix the flour, baking powder, sugar, spice and walnuts together.

4. In a separate bowl mix the prunes, cooking liquid, oil and egg.

5. Fold together the flour mixture and the prune mixture, adding orange juice to give a soft consistency.

6. Put into a greased and lined 900g/2lb loaf tin.

7. Decorate with walnuts.

8. Bake at 170°C/325°F/Gas Mark 3 for 1¼ hours.

TIME: Preparation takes 15 minutes, cooking takes 1¼ hours.

FREEZING: Freeze after cooking for up to 2 months.

FRUIT CAKE

This cake freezes well.

MAKES 1 CAKE

350g/12oz plain wholemeal flour
1 tsp mixed spice
1½ tsps bicarbonate of soda
175g/6oz margarine
175g/6oz demerara sugar
175g/6oz currants
75g/3oz sultanas
½ pint soya milk
1 tbsp lemon juice

1. Sift the flour, spice and bicarbonate of soda together into a large bowl.

2. Rub in the fat until the mixture resembles fine breadcrumbs.

3. Add the sugar, currants and sultanas.

4. Mix the milk and lemon juice together and add to the dry ingredients.

5. Mix well to form a dropping consistency.

6. Leave the mixture overnight.

7. Turn into a prepared 25cm x 12cm/10" x 5" tin.

8. Bake in the centre of the oven at 160°C/325°F/Gas Mark 3 for 2 hours.

TIME: Preparation takes 20 minutes, cooking takes 2 hours.

VARIATION: Use sour milk in place of the milk/lemon mixture.

OATMEAL AND TREACLE SCONES

A tasty alternative to plain scones.

MAKES ABOUT 12 SCONES

100g/4oz plain wholemeal flour
2 level tsps baking powder
Pinch of salt
25g/1oz margarine
100g/4oz oatmeal
1 tbsp molasses
Milk to bind

1. Sieve the flour, baking powder and salt into a bowl three times.

2. Rub in the margarine, then add the oatmeal.

3. Warm the molasses and 1 tbsp of the milk.

4. Bind the flour mixture with the molasses and milk, adding extra milk as necessary.

5. Roll out to 0.6cm/¼ " thick and cut into 5cm/2" rounds.

6. Bake on a greased baking sheet at 220°C/425°F/Gas Mark 7 for 10 minutes.

7. Remove and place on a wire rack to cool.

TIME: Preparation takes 10 minutes, cooking takes 10 minutes.

FREEZING: The scones may be placed in a freezer bag or container and frozen after cooking.

INDEX